Milperra

Milperra

THE ROAD
TO JUSTICE

RON STEPHENSON

NEW
HOLLAND

This edition published in 2022 by New Holland Publishers
First published in 2004 by New Holland Publishers
Sydney

Level 1, 178 Fox Valley Road, Wahroonga, NSW 2076, Australia

newhollandpublishers.com

Copyright © 2004 New Holland Publishers
Copyright © 2004 in text: Ron Stephenson

Cover photograph courtesy of New Ltd and photographer Ian Mainsbridge,
all other photographs Ron Stephenson and the *Australian Police Journal*

A record of this book is held at the National Library of Australia.

ISBN 9781760794781

Managing Director: Fiona Schultz
Project Editor: Glenda Downing
Designer: Andrew Davies
Production Director: Arlene Gippert
Printed in Australia by SOS Print + Media Group

10 9 8 7 6 5 4 3 2 1

Keep up with New Holland Publishers:

 NewHollandPublishers

 @newhollandpublishers

To playwright John Misto
for his encouragement

CONTENTS

ACKNOWLEDGEMENTS

Many thanks for the efforts and professionalism of Selwa Anthony and the staff of New Holland Publishers, in particular my editor Glenda Downing, whose confidence in me made it possible for this story to be told.

INTRODUCTION

Recently I read a newspaper article announcing that *Moulin Rouge* producer Martin Brown would be making a movie about the Milperra Massacre. The article quoted Brown as saying, 'People like the idea of a biker flick. There hasn't been one for a while – a powerful, hard core, rock'n'roll biker film. The film views the massacre in which seven people died in a shoot-out between rival bikie clubs in 1984.'

The article was referring, of course, to the infamous Father's Day bikie massacre at Milperra in Sydney's south, between two outlaw motorcycle gangs, the Comanchero and the Bandidos.

When I read the producer's enthusiastic words, I wondered how any film could possibly tell the truth about what happened. So much of what went on at Milperra, before and after the slaughter, has remained a well-kept secret up to this day.

Although a lot has been written about the 'Father's Day Massacre', almost nothing is known about how the bikies were finally brought to justice. The daunting and perilous task that confronted the NSW Police Force is one of the great untold stories of Australian criminal history. The massacre was to change the lives of everyone caught up in it.

The real events of that day have since been clouded with myth and rumour – with a large gap existing between the hype and reality. It is unlikely that any film, however well intentioned, could bridge that gap.

I made a decision to fill that void before Hollywood distorted the story forever. I would write about those events, honestly and factually, from an insider's point of view.

On Father's Day 1984, I was at Milperra. I counted the dead. I photographed their bodies. And I led the team that finally brought their killers to justice.

This is our story.

CHAPTER ONE

A Double Threat

True stories have quite different beginnings from fictional tales. A person with a fertile imagination can invent a suitable introduction for a fictional novel. Not so with a true story. In that case, the script has already been written and needs only to be told. An appropriate starting point has to be determined. The correct time to commence this story is June 1984, when a totally different crime from that of Milperra took place: the attempted murder of Sydney detective Mick Drury. The book *Line of Fire* and the film *Blue Murder* both relate the story behind that crime. My story tells a different, insider's point of view, with parallels that run with the Milperra Bikie Massacre. June 1984 saw the birth of the blackest era in the history of the NSW Police Force and that of the outlaw bikie gangs.

Detective Senior Constable Michael Drury was an undercover agent attached to the NSW Police Drug Squad. At 6 pm on 6 June, Drury was shot twice by an unknown offender at his Chatswood home in Sydney's north. He was critically wounded and admitted to Royal North Shore Hospital. There the detective hovered between life and death for many weeks and was not expected to survive. The weapon used was believed to be a .38 calibre Smith and Wesson revolver.

I was performing late shift supervisory duties that evening as the detective inspector 'on call' for any serious investigations. I called into the Drug Squad office to offer assistance, but the shooting was being treated with the urgency that was required by senior officers of the Drug Squad and my assistance was not needed.

A motive for the shooting appeared to come from a drug bust that Drury had been involved with during the preceding two years. In March 1982, Drury, acting as an undercover agent, participated in two arrests in Melbourne of criminals Robert Jack Richardson and Brian Carl Hansen. A third offender, Allan Williams aka McClure, escaped the police raid. He was later arrested and charged similarly to the other two with possession of a considerable amount of heroin. The strength of the case against Williams lay in his identification by Drury.

Richardson and Hansen were committed to stand trial in Victoria, but Williams was discharged by the magistrate. Drury was unhappy about that decision and made strong representations to the Victorian Attorney-General for an ex-officio indictment to be filed against Williams. This application was successful and Williams was ordered to stand trial alongside his two brothers in crime.

Apart from Mick Drury, Richardson and Hansen were also in a position to give evidence against Williams. In March 1984, Richardson's body was found beside a Victorian road with two bullet holes to the head.

Two of the players who could convict Williams by their evidence had been taken out of the picture: Richardson was dead and Michael Drury lay critically wounded in hospital. Whoever was responsible was playing for keeps.

At that time, I was a detective inspector in command of the Regional Crime Squad South, a regional arm of the Criminal Investigation Branch (CIB) operating from Miranda to the south of Sydney. On the evening of 11 July 1984, five weeks after the shooting of Drury, I was telephoned at my home by Detective Superintendent Angus McDonald who was the officer-in-charge of Operations at the CIB. He was also the acting chief of the CIB because of the retirement of the permanent commander. Angus informed me that I was required to meet him at the CIB in Sydney at 7 am the following day to assist him in a 'nasty' inquiry. The nature of that investigation would be revealed when I saw him.

When I met Angus he told me that a startling development had arisen in the Drury shooting. He had interviewed the wounded detective in hospital and was informed that Detective Sergeant Roger Rogerson, stationed at Darlinghurst, had offered Drury a bribe of between $15,000 and $25,000 if he could assist a criminal named Williams who Drury had arrested on a drug matter.

To complicate the matter, a detective from Newcastle had come to the CIB with information that he said was crucial to the Drury shooting. An informant had told him that Drury was corrupt, that he associated with criminals and prostitutes and was having an affair with a barmaid named Sandra Lee aka Everett who worked at the White Horse Hotel in Camperdown, an inner west Sydney suburb. Prior to working at the White Horse, she had worked at The George Hotel in St Kilda, Victoria. Inquiries made to the publicans at both hotels failed to identify any person of that name having worked for them.

Superintendent McDonald had earlier made arrangements to have a Dying Deposition taken from Drury at his hospital bedside, so critical was his condition. Magistrate Mr John Abernethy, assisted by the senior police prosecutor Superintendent Sweeney, would officiate.

At 11.30 am on 12 July 1984, I was at Mick Drury's bedside when Angus McDonald had the following conversation with him.

'I have arranged for a magistrate to be here shortly to obtain a deposition about what you told me yesterday.'

'Superintendent, what I told you yesterday is the truth. So help me God,' replied Drury in a voice racked with pain.

'As a result of what we have been told, there are some matters requiring clarification. Firstly, do you know a prostitute named Sandra Lee or Everett?' asked Angus.

'No. Am I supposed to have arrested her?' answered Drury.

'No. Her name has been mentioned in our inquiries and there have been suggestions that you had a relationship with a woman of that name,' said McDonald.

'I have never heard of her and do not know her. I am a happily married man and have no relationships,' was Drury's reply.

Mr Abernethy arrived and the deposition was taken. I left the hospital with McDonald. Drury did not die. He remained in hospital for many weeks, but he did survive.

To verify the information supplied by the 'gig', or informer, of the Newcastle detective, McDonald and I travelled to the northern city and met him at an RSL club. During our car trip to the meeting, Angus said to me, 'Do you know much about bikie gangs?'

'A little. Not too much. Why do you ask?'

'I got a whisper from a mate at the BCI (Bureau of Crime Intelligence), that two gangs going under the names of Comanchero and Bandidos are heading for a blue. There've been a couple of hits already,' he said.

'What's happening about it?' I asked.

'Nothing yet. The intelligence crowd say they are keeping an eye on it,' was his reply.

We arrived in Newcastle, putting the bikies out of our minds. More important matters were on our plate. But Angus's words would prove to be prophetic: 'they're heading for a blue'.

The informant identified himself to us as Patrick Terrence Wallace. He was under committal to stand trial on a charge of armed robbery. Wallace wanted a monetary reward and assistance with his court case in return for information he could give the police regarding the shooting of Detective Drury.

He then related a story of utter garbage, which when condensed amounted to nothing more than a story that he had manufactured, suggesting that Drury was corrupt, had associated improperly with the Painters and Dockers in Melbourne and had an adulterous relationship with Sandra Lee. He suggested that the shooting would have emanated from his conduct in one of these areas. All of these so-called motives were blown out of the water before we left the club. Wallace was full of crap.

Over the next six weeks McDonald and I interviewed many witnesses, police and civilian, in relation to Mick Drury's revelation that Roger Rogerson had offered him a bribe. Information confirmed that Rogerson had spoken to Drury in the early part of 1983 at Darlinghurst Police Station. Rogerson had arranged the meeting. Drury claimed that he was spoken to about 'the Melbourne matter' and Rogerson said to him, 'If the right thing is done for Williams in Melbourne, you will get fifteen to twentyfive thousand.'

Drury said that he rejected the suggestion, saying that he wanted nothing to do with it. He intended to go to Melbourne and give his evidence truthfully and fully.

McDonald and I interviewed Rogerson. He denied any impropriety. He offered the name of an old false pretender named William Mair, whom he claimed he had met in the street and told Rogerson that if he knew Drury he should let him know to watch his back as a lot of money had been paid by Williams to beat the charge. That was why he had arranged the meeting with Drury.

One day during the inquiry, Angus again returned to the subject of the bad blood between the bikies. The Comanchero and Bandidos were so hostile towards each other that any time their paths crossed there would be violence. A close watch was being kept, but by whom? Intelligence officers are not operational police officers and would simply file their information away in a cabinet. Angus and I received a fair bit of 'lip-service' or near truths from witnesses during our attempt to establish the truth of Drury's allegations. No one, however, came forward with any information to support Mick's claim. Drury had been on his deathbed and had nothing to achieve by making a claim of being offered a bribe. He thought that the reason for his attempted murder lay behind that offer. I had to agree with him. Rogerson, on the other hand, may have had good reason to deny the accusation.

Confirmation of that may have come in the form of a threat. Towards the end of our inquiry, I was at my office in the Miranda Crime Squad when Angus rang me.

'Will you meet me in half an hour at Brighton? Outside Le Sands Restaurant. Do you know it?'

'Yes. I'll be there.'

Angus was already there when I arrived. When I sat in his car I saw that he was very distressed. Angus was a deep thinker and a proud Scotsman.

'What's up, mate?' I asked.

He didn't answer straight away. I knew he would when he was ready. Finally he said, 'I've been threatened. A fellow rang me and said if I didn't go easy on this inquiry, he'd ruin my career. He's got nothing on me. I'm just letting you know what has happened. I am a superintendent of police and I will do my job. You may hear about this threat, but don't think that it has changed me. I am committed to this inquiry and will not be told what to do.'

I could not believe what Angus had just told me and I asked, 'Who made the threat?'

'That doesn't matter. It's bullshit,' he answered.

On 16 August 1984, our completed joint file was submitted to the Commissioner of Police. Without further evidence, no recommendation for action to be taken against Rogerson could be made. A further inquiry, made by other police, would be conducted some time later, when lips opened and supported Drury. But that's another story.

The shooting of Mick Drury and allegations that a brother police officer may have been associated with the crime, created a black day in the history of the NSW Police Force.

The time span of Angus McDonald and my inquiry was from June 1984 through to the end of August that year. This time frame coincided with the approach of another criminal episode that would shock the nation. While a concentration of police interest had centred on the Drury shooting, a build-up of aggression between two outlaw bikie gangs had reached explosion point. Angus had been right. Police intelligence had monitored its growth, but that was as far as it went. Just a prediction.

CHAPTER TWO

Signal One

The passenger lounge of the international airport in Sydney was crowded with people either leaving on flights or with those who had come to farewell them. On this occasion, I was the one waving goodbye.

Angus McDonald and his wife were leaving Sydney for a two-month holiday in the United Kingdom. Apart from being my boss, Angus was also my friend. His wife too had become a friend, a lawyer by profession and later to become Governor of Queensland.

We had taken our inquiry into the shooting of Mick Drury as far as we could and were both looking forward to a break. Angus was starting his annual leave and, the following day, Sunday 2 September 1984, was my last day of duty before I started my own leave. Or so I thought. If I had known what lay ahead, I might have joined him on that flight. A heavy responsibility would fall on my shoulders. One that would etch an indelible mark into Australia's criminal history.

* * *

Father's Day 1984 fell on Sunday 2 September. I was being treated to a barbecue with my family at the home of my daughter Louise at Bonnet Bay, a southern Sydney suburb. The weather was perfect, a lovely spring day in Sydney and we soaked up the sunshine as we sat around the swimming pool. I hoped that the weather was a forerunner to the start of my impending holidays. I was 53 years old, had been married for 30 years and a NSW Police officer for 33 years. My son who was a serving NSW Police officer and two married daughters made up the immediate family.

Father's Day brought with it the usual gifts from the family: socks, a shirt, a tie and a bottle of good scotch. The company, though, was more important. A family growing up with a father as an operational police officer shared their time with interruptions that created long hours of separation during crime investigations. Days such as Father's Day were special.

About 1.15 pm, Louise came from inside the house and said, 'Dad, you're wanted on the phone. Don't be too long. The steaks are nearly ready.'

These mundane words started a life-changing experience.

A roster system operated within the Criminal Investigation Branch that ensured a commissioned officer was available to be 'called out' to any serious crime or occurrence. That officer would attend the scene of the crime and assess the situation. If necessary, he would arrange for any further assistance. I was the duty officer on call that day and had to inform the police radio where I could be contacted. The police radio is the nerve centre of the department and is situated in the Sydney Police Centre. At any one time there would be a staff of ten on duty, supervised by an inspector.

'Is that Inspector Stephenson?' asked the male voice at the other end of the line.

'Yes,' I replied. 'Who's that?'

'This is the police radio, boss. I'm a bit uncertain at this time, but there's been a few calls on this one. There's a man gone berserk with a rifle at the Viking Tavern at Milperra and a few shots have been fired.' 'I'll head out there. Keep me informed and let me know if I'm not needed,' were my parting words to the radio operator.

Bad luck about lunch, I thought to myself as I changed into my street clothes. I had remembered to bring everything except a belt. Peter, my son-in-law, had a 32 inch waist and mine was a 36, but one borrowed from him was the best I could do. A bit tight, but it wouldn't be for long, or so I thought at the time. A five-shot .38 calibre Smith and Wesson revolver fitted snugly into a leather shoulder holster which completed my mufti uniform.

'A bit of trouble at Milperra. I shouldn't be too long. Sorry about the steaks, but save me one,' was my quick goodbye to the family.

They showed no surprise. Father's Day without Dad – just another one of those interruptions.

Bonnet Bay was a comfortable 30-minute drive from Milperra and I travelled at a leisurely pace in the unmarked police car that carried the departmental radio call sign of CI–130. I used the radio handset to call VKG, the police radio, and said, 'CI–130. Can you give me directions to the job at Milperra? I'm coming from the Menai area.'

'Get into Henry Lawson Drive, turn up River Road and go through Revesby. Beaconsfield Street then runs off to your left. I confirm that shots have been fired.'

I travelled down the S-bends of River Road to the narrow Menai Bridge crossing the Woronora River. Standing alongside the bridge, protruding from the river, were a number of pylons that would eventually carry a new, multi-laned road and remove the never-ending traffic bottleneck.

Menai had languished quietly over the years as a backwater, but was now giving way to a population expansion bringing with it shops, a hotel, schools and modern, two-storey homes. The suburb was originally named Bangor, but in 1910 was renamed Menai. Apart from being one of the oldest settlements in the Sutherland Shire, it was becoming one of the fastest growing areas.

A crackling message from the police radio receiver took my mind off any further sightseeing.

'Cars attending the Viking Tavern at Milperra. It has been reported as an armed hold-up. One person has been shot.'

I pressed the accelerator a little harder towards the floor and climbed the hills of Menai Road to Illawarra Road and headed towards Alfords Point Bridge spanning the Georges River.

'Car 19–10. I'm off at the location. I can see a man with a rifle leaning across the roof of a Holden. I'll keep back until backup arrives,' came the voice through the radio. He was a uniformed officer from the Bankstown Police Patrol.

Then, from the same officer, 'It's a Signal One situation.'

Some years earlier a code book had been designed and introduced by the department to thwart the ever-intrusive media but was dropped when the media obtained a copy. Various signal numbers represented different crimes. Signal 18 meant murder, Signal 48 assault. Signal One, however, was the most important and was still used by police. It meant 'constable in trouble'. Whenever Signal One was broadcast, every police officer dropped what they were doing and responded to the call.

I pushed the accelerator flat to the floor and activated the car's siren for quicker access on the narrow, two-laned road. I felt like a stunt driver as cars parted in front of me to allow me through.

Polair2, the police eye in the sky, had been refuelling at nearby Bankstown Airport and was soon above the Viking Tavern. The crew of the helicopter were able to describe the scene below and relay their information to the police cars screaming towards the tavern.

Their assessment was that hundreds of bikies had gathered in the car park of the tavern. Several of them were armed with firearms, which were being discharged. Many people had gathered at the rear entrance of the hotel, attempting to escape from the danger. This was no armed hold-up, but a battle.

Car CI–132 was attached to my command at the Regional Crime Squad, Miranda, and contained a number of officers from the Armed Hold-Up Unit who were also SWOS trained. SWOS was the Special Weapons Operations Squad who had been trained in the use of multiple types of weapons and in hostage negotiations. They too had heard the call for assistance and were on their way. In fact, they were only a short distance in front of me. Detective Sergeant Trevor Baker was the senior officer on board and I heard his voice over the radio.

'This is CI–132. We have SWOS personnel on board. Ask Car 19–10 and the other cars to remain out of the car park and set up a perimeter to isolate the crime scene.'

The other police cars complied with the request and the area was soon isolated. But the fighting between the bikies continued.

I had reached Beaconsfield Street and could see the flashing blue and red lights of police and emergency vehicles ahead. Screeching to a halt at the police barrier, I got out of the car cautiously, my revolver now in hand.

A decision had been made by the SWOS officers just minutes before my arrival to enter the isolation zone, restore order and allow the ambulance crews to treat the injured. Uniformed police were now pouring into the Esso Service Station opposite the pub. They were disarming bikies who had spilled from the hotel car park in the thick of armed battle. Shots were still being fired in the car park and the acrid smell of gunpowder filled the air.

I looked towards the hotel and saw one of my SWOS officers, John Garvey, a detective senior constable, standing face-to-face with an offender armed with a shotgun. Garvey also held a shotgun and was wearing a bulletproof vest. The offender was wearing a bikie's gang jacket with the name 'Comanchero' printed in capital letters across the back. The detective edged closer to the bikie who had blood running from the left side of his face where he had earlier been struck by a shotgun pellet. Garvey pushed aside the shotgun and wrenched it from the hands of Raymond 'Sunshine' Kucler.

Other fights were taking place in the grounds of the hotel and shouts of anger were audible. Injured bikies, victims of the conflict, were being punched, thumped and abused by their enemies as they were carried on stretchers to waiting ambulances. People were sheltering behind cars, trees, anything that offered safety. Screams of terror were mixed with the shouts of anger and abuse. Both uniformed and plainclothes police grappled with the bikies, disarming them.

I had fixed my ID shield into the top pocket of my coat. The ID consisted of a silver badge fitted onto a red background card, red signifying the rank of inspector. A detective ran up to me and shouted, 'It's a war between Bandidos and Comanchero.'

After ten minutes the gunshots finally ceased as the fighting abated and the police gained control. I took a quick look at the scene. The car park was large, about 75 square metres, containing approximately 500 people, most dressed in leather jackets with varying coloured logos. Motorcycles, sedans and utility vans filled the area, leaving just enough space for stalls, which held motor vehicle spare parts and barbecue stands. What had begun as a market day for selling motor bike accessories had turned into a battlefield.

At my feet lay the body of a Bandidos bikie. I was to learn that his name was Gregory Campbell, known by his gang name of 'Shadow'. He had been shot in the face with a load of shotgun pellets and his face was covered in blood. Shadow's Bandidos brother and real-life sibling, Phillip 'Bull' Campbell, lay across his body, heaving and sobbing with sadness and anger.

I could see other bodies lying in the car park. Some order had to be established. I was the senior police officer and had to assume control. The book of police rules and instructions, the police bible, didn't cover a situation like this when advising officers on how to perform and what they should do. I'm sure if the manual could speak, it would firstly shrug and then say, 'Do your best'.

Word passes quickly among police officers about who is in command, the one with whom 'the buck stops'. Some are relieved that it is not their turn to accept responsibility. It had happened to me before and no doubt would again. I always wondered why these officers wanted senior positions but they were not prepared to accept the responsibility that went with the job. However, of the two hundred plus police officers in attendance at the scene, one officer was in command and would be responsible for his decisions. And he could only be successful with the full support of his junior officers.

I was joined by several senior non-commissioned officers (NCOs) or detective sergeants from the CIB. Among them was Jim Counsel. He had been enjoying his annual leave and Father's Day celebrations at his home when he heard of the battle over a commercial radio station. He dropped his knife and fork and drove his own car to the tavern to give assistance.

'Stick close to me, Jim,' I said, pleased to see him there. 'Help me to arrange some order here.'

It wouldn't be easy. The air was filled with anger, panic and apprehension. Jim was attached to the Homicide Squad of the CIB and was experienced in murder investigations. His know-how would be invaluable. Of the other NCOs, I assembled a group of competent detective sergeants from the CIB who would form my command.

Barry Smith (Homicide) would be my second-in-command and liaison officer. Aarne Tees (Homicide) was selected to investigate the Comanchero's involvement in the massacre and their background. Bill Duff (Homicide) was to perform similar duties in respect to the Bandidos. Darryl Wilson (Homicide) would act as a supervisor with Jim Counsel.

My first responsibility was to protect the crime scene from contamination. This was no easy task, since frantic relatives and the media were arriving in droves. We decided to form an outer perimeter of uniformed officers to restrain onlookers, the news media and all unauthorised persons. Next we established an inner perimeter with crime scene tape to contain possible offenders, witnesses, weaponry, motor vehicles and the bodies of those killed.

We could not move them until they had been photographed and examined by the coroner.

A mobile command post in the form of a caravan arrived at the scene, brought there by members of the NSW Police Radio and Electronics Unit. The vehicle was equipped with a police radio base station, portable radios, telephones, whiteboards, torches and every conceivable item that could be required for use in an emergency situation. Importantly, there was also a director's chair, from where the commander could issue his orders and receive their results. It was a place where every officer knew that he could contact his leader.

The hotel continued to trade and business was suddenly very brisk as patrons stood with schooners of beer in their hands surveying the scene before them. They had ringside seats. The publican was advised to close down his service as boozed-up bikies would not help the inquiry.

But what had gone on here? Why had two bikie gangs suddenly turned on each other?

A story began to unfold as witnesses were interviewed. A bikie swap meeting had been organised that day by the British Motorcycle Club. Most of the Sydney motorcycling fraternity attended, being represented by biker clubs and outlaw bikie gangs or OMGs. OMGs are bikie clubs that disregard the law.

Five hundred people packed into the large car park of the Viking Tavern with another two hundred crammed into the bars in the hotel. Barbecues in the car park prepared and provided food for the participants. Stalls displayed spare motor vehicle parts for sale, new, second-hand and some 'hot'.

The Comanchero and Bandidos had gone to the hotel not for a swap meet, but for a full-scale armed war. They were both OMGs, also known as 'one-per-centers', because one per cent of all citizens who own and ride motorcycles choose anarchy as a lifestyle. They had degenerated into disruptive and dangerous criminal tribes. A '1%' patch worn on the gang jacket, or Colours, indicated their calling.

The Bandidos originated in Houston, Texas, in 1966 and promoted themselves under that name. The name was inspired by 'Frito Bandido', a popular fictional figure in television commercials in the United States. He was depicted as a fat Mexican dressed in a serape, wearing a large, straw sombrero and holding a machete in one hand and a revolver in the other. 'Frito' was adopted as the Bandidos' logo and was worn in the centre back of the members' Colours – usually a leather or denim jacket.

The Bandidos' membership grew in size to become accredited in the United States by the Federal Bureau of Investigation (FBI) as one of the 'Big Four' of outlaw motorcycle gangs alongside the Hells Angels, Outlaws and Pagans.

The Comanchero had a different and slightly more eccentric origin. In 1968, an enigmatic Scotsman named William George 'Jock' Ross organised the formation of a Sydney-based outlaw motorcycle gang named the Comanchero after an early John Wayne movie. Their Colours were fashioned from a white falcon hovering over a motorcycle wheel with the word 'Comanchero' printed in yellow in the shape of a horseshoe.

Their clubhouse was initially at Birchgrove and later at 65 Harris Street, Harris Park, in Sydney's residential western suburbs. Membership grew and all members swore adherence to the Comanchero law: 'As the Brotherhood of the Comanchero is run on a paramilitary basis and not as a "do as you like" social club, the following laws must be absolutely obeyed...' Their own Ten Commandments were then drawn up as the club rules, with Jock in the role of Moses:

1. THE PRESIDENT IS THE SUPREME COMMANDER OF THE COMANCHERO.
2. ANY MEMBER FOUND GUILTY OF COWARDICE WILL BE THROWN OUT OF THE CLUB.

3. ANY MEMBER FOUND GUILTY OF STEALING FROM A MEMBER OF THE CLUB ITSELF WILL BE THROWN OUT OF THE CLUB.

4. ANY MEMBER FOUND GUILTY OF SCREWING ANOTHER MEMBER'S REAL OL' LADY OR TAKING ADVANTAGE OF A RIFT BETWEEN THEM FOR FUTURE 'CONNING-UP' WILL BE THROWN OUT.

5. ANY MEMBER FOUND GUILTY OF BREEDING DISSENSION IN THE CLUB (I.E. RUNNING DOWN THE PRESIDENT OF THE CLUB OR CLUB POLICIES IN ANY WAY, SHAPE OR FORM – OR BAD SHIT RUMOURS) WILL BE THROWN OUT.

6. ANY MEMBER FOUND GUILTY OF SELLING, DISTRIBUTING OR USING HARD DRUGS WILL BE THROWN OUT.

7. ANY MEMBER FOUND GUILTY OF USING THEIR SUPERIOR ABILITY TO 'CON' ANOTHER MEMBER OR NOMINATED MEMBER OUT OF THEIR BIKES, MONEY OR VALUABLES WILL BE SEVERELY DEALT WITH.

8. ANY MEMBER FOUND GUILTY OF NOT HELPING ANOTHER MEMBER WHO IS IN GENUINE TROUBLE, NOT BULLSHIT TROUBLE, WILL BE SEVERELY DEALT WITH.

9. ANY MEMBER FOUND GUILTY OF DIVULGING CLUB BUSINESS TO ANYONE NOT A MEMBER, UNLESS DIRECTED BY THE PRESIDENT, WILL BE SEVERELY DEALT WITH.

10. ANY MEMBER FOUND GUILTY OF WEARING HIS COLOURS ON OR IN ANYTHING OTHER THAN A BRITISH OR AMERICAN MOTORCYCLE OF 500CC OR MORE, WILL BE SEVERELY DEALT WITH.

The use of firearms was also spelled out to the gang members.

REGULATIONS FOR FIREARMS
FAILURE TO ABIDE BY THESE REGULATIONS WILL RESULT IN SEVERE DISCIPLINARY ACTION BY JOCK.

1. NO WOMAN WILL HANDLE ANY FIREARM FOR ANY TRIVIAL REASON.

2. FIREARMS WILL NOT BE HANDLED BY ANYONE EXCEPT THE OWNER OR AUTHORISED PERSON BY THE OWNER.

3. NO OWNER WILL BE PERMITTED TO HANDLE HIS OWN WEAPON IF HE IS DRUNK.

4. NO FIREARM IS TO BE DISCHARGED IN THE CLUBHOUSE, GROUNDS OR SURROUNDING GROUNDS.

5. NO FIREARM IS TO HAVE A SHELL IN THE BREECH.

NATURALLY IF THE CLUBHOUSE IS ATTACKED, THE ABOVE-MENTIONED REGULATIONS WILL NOT APPLY.

The gang prospered under Jock's command until 1983, when several members became dissatisfied with his autocratic style and his distaste for the easy money available in the drug business. Anthony Mark 'Snoddy' Spencer and Charles Paul 'Charlie' Scibberas deserted the gang and burned their Colours. This was an unforgivable act.

The two renegades travelled to Houston and spoke with the President and officers of the mother chapter of the Bandidos. Like any legitimate business, they were seeking to acquire a franchise to form a Sydney chapter of the gang and to engage in some commercial activity. Permission was given by the Americans, and Snoddy Spencer and Charlie Scibberas returned to Sydney to establish the Australian arm of the Bandidos. This decision would be the genesis of the Viking Tavern war.

The Bandidos converted a cottage at 150 Louisa Street, Birchgrove, into their clubhouse. This was the former home of the now depleted Comanchero. It was situated in an up-market residential area of Sydney. Motorcycle engine noises and other disturbing sounds echoed from the building at all hours of the day, annoying residents of the trendy neighbourhood. Nobody, however, dared to complain.

Snoddy elected himself as President and began recruiting members. Some of them defected from the Comanchero, looking for the excitement of a new bikie life. The Bandidos membership soon gathered numbers and a formidable outlaw motorcycle gang was created.

The by-laws of the parent chapter in Texas were adopted, which described how the gang should be formed. Their members must be at least 18 years of age and would serve a six-month probation period. Members of the Sydney chapter would elect their executive officers: President, Vice President, Secretary, Treasurer, Sergeant at Arms and Road Captain. Each member was permitted to have an honorary member, his woman, referred to as his 'Ol' Lady'. The motorcycle, the gang member's pride, should be 500cc capacity or greater.

Patches worn on a Bandidos' Colours signified different things about the wearer. These patches would also indicate to the observer how serious a bikie the wearer was. 'BFFB' was for Bandido Forever, Forever Bandido, and 'MC' meant a motorcycle club, not a street gang.

The Bandidos designed their personal calling card. In the centre were the words 'Courtesy Card – Bandidos' above a drawing of the fat Mexican. Below the logo were the words 'We are the people our parents warned us about – if you can't be well liked, be well hated.' Yet there was no such thing as a stereotypical bikie among these men. And during the investigation of the massacre we were to learn that it was a mistake to think of them all as scruffy, puerile misfits. Indeed, we were astounded to discover that their line of work ranged from long-term unemployment to truck driver, pay clerk, cleaner, marine engineer, optical mechanic and a clerk with 15 years' service in the NSW Department of Lands. Another member had managed a family plumbing business for 25 years. Again we were astonished to discover that one of them even played classical piano.

What drove these men to such a way of life?

The bitterness between the Bandidos and Comanchero grew to such an extent that on 10 August 1984 a bikie war was declared.

The Presidents of both gangs spoke abrasively to each other over the telephone. The war declaration was officially ratified.

There were not too many rules governing the campaign. A bikie could not be hit at his home or place of employment, otherwise it was open slather. If ever the two gangs met, a full-scale armed confrontation could be expected. The bikies armed themselves in readiness for the inevitable bloodshed that accompanies any war.

CHAPTER THREE

The Hit List

Time ran out. A peaceful resolution of the gangs' problems could not be found. The swap meeting at the Viking Tavern was the ideal battleground. An audience of brother bikies could witness the triumph of the superior gang.

At 1 pm on Sunday 2 September 1984, Father's Day, the Comanchero filtered into the crowded car park where the swap meeting was under way. They were dressed in their Colours of a white falcon atop a red motorcycle wheel with the word 'Comanchero' in yellow printed in the shape of a horseshoe. They communicated with each other by walkie-talkie radio. Each bikie was armed with a firearm, chain, knife, baseball bat, iron bar or knuckle dusters. They waited.

The residents of Beaconsfield Street, Milperra, were fascinated by a distant humming sound, like that of a hive of droning bees. As the noise came closer it grew more distinct as 30 members of a bikie convoy proceed towards the Viking Tavern. It was now 1.15 pm. The bikies, in wedge-shaped formation, turned into the entrance of the car park of the Viking Tavern. The Bandidos outlaw bikie gang had arrived to sort out their differences with the Comanchero.

Many of the riders' machines had scabbards fixed across the handlebars holding rifles and shotguns. Those who were not armed went to the gang's utility van, the 'war wagon', where they selected their weapons.

The Bandidos, dressed in their Colours of the fat Mexican garbed in a serape and sombrero, and armed with machetes and revolvers, advanced into the crowded car park. The Comanchero stood in the crowd, holding their weapons in the combat position. President William Jock Ross raised a machete with the words 'Bandaid Hair Parter' painted on it and led his men with the shout, 'Kill 'em all'.

The battle began. The main war raged for 20 minutes. Bats, iron bars, guns, knives, batons, chains and machetes were used, gang against gang, brother against brother. The warriors, some bearded, their plaited hair held back by colourful headbands and bandanas, dressed in jeans, studded leather gloves and displaying their beloved gang's Colours, fought for victory and supremacy.

People screamed, people ran, people hid. Shotgun pellets peppered victims and the shots that missed their target smacked into buildings, motor vehicles and fences. Bandidos, Comanchero and bystanders were struck. Limbs were broken, people were stabbed, people were shot, people died.

As the news of the massacre spread across the VKG police radio network, patrolling police sped to the Viking Tavern. The Signal One call brought highway patrol officers, detectives, uniformed general duties police, Tactical Response Group members and specialised weapons officers from the Special Weapons Operations Squad to the scene. Off-duty police officers like Jim Counsel rushed to the Tavern to offer assistance in quelling the battle.

The Blue Line had entered the battlefield and won control over the warring bikies who were still holding smoking firearms and bloodstained baseball bats. In the 20 minutes of fierce bikie fighting, four Comanchero, two Bandidos and a 14-year-old girl had been killed. Twenty-one people, mostly bikies from the two gangs, received serious injuries that required hospital treatment.

Police scientific experts from the Scientific Branch had the unenviable duty of examining, searching and photographing the deceased. I had with me a 35mm camera which I had intended to take family snaps with at my Father's Day barbecue. It would now be used for a far different purpose. There is nothing like a photograph taken at the time to accurately record a crime scene. As the specialists took their photographs for evidential purposes, I took mine to forever remind me of that bloodbath.

The majority of people who are shot when they are standing fall to the ground on their faces. The bodies of the dead were rolled onto their backs to reveal their faces, frozen in a grim, smiling death mask. I walked with three of the Scientific examiners through the crime scene, photographing as we moved between the two hundred motor vehicles. Most were motorcycles; the Harley Davidson, the close relative of the bikie. Scabbards, baton holders and gun holsters were strapped to the machines. Alongside them lay the dead and injured.

Sergeant Brian Murchie, a seasoned, street-hardened uniformed police officer, said to a probationary constable, 'Have a good look around here, son. You won't see anything like this again.' I thought that his comment could well have been directed to me.

At the entrance to the car park, on the footpath verge of Beaconsfield Street, I saw the body of 'Shadow' Campbell, the Bandidos' Vice President. He had taken a shotgun load to his face. Carried there by his Bandidos brothers 'Gloves' McElwaine and 'Tiny' Cain, they had lain him down as he gurgled and drowned in his own blood.

In his wallet, Campbell carried a false driver's licence with the name of another bikie, James John Posar of Marion Street, Leichhardt. Posar, however, was well and truly alive.

Nearby, also in the car park, was the body of Mario 'Chopper' Cianter. He had been rolled onto his back. His eyes were open, but sightless. Blood had run from his mouth and was now drying where it had flowed into his beard. A load of shotgun pellets had shattered his chest through the emblem '1%–Bandidos–Australia', which he had worn with pride before he was killed. The 'Death Before Dishonour' tattoo on his arm seemed prophetic.

Between two Harley Davidson motorbikes lay Robert 'Foghorn' Lane, the Vice President of the Comanchero. He had fallen victim to a .357 magnum rifle blast to the centre of his chest. He died where he fell. A search of Foghorn's wallet revealed a driver's licence in the fictitious name of John Simon Carlton of Harris Park. Like many a man before entering battle, Foghorn had had a premonition of death. On the preceding night he had wisely drawn up a will.

Tony 'Dog' McCoy lay nearby with his eyes staring unblinkingly at the sky. His face was covered in blood where the shotgun pellets had struck. His Comanchero Colours were pelted with shot while his left hand, covered by a studded, black leather glove, clutched vainly at his chest.

A short distance away, next to a barbecue stand, lay his brother Comanchero, Phillip 'Leroy' Jeske, the gang's Sergeant at Arms. He had been hit in the back by a single shot from a .357 Rossi rifle. The bullet had passed through his body and exited through the Sergeant at Arms patch worn on the left breast of his Colours. His sunglasses no longer served their purpose of shading his eyes from the sun. Leroy also had a false driver's licence, in the name of Terrence William Parker from Forster.

The fourth dead Comanchero, Ivan 'Sparrow' Romcek, had been shot at such close range that wadding from a spent cartridge had embedded in his neck. He had numerous shotgun pellets in his left upper chest, right shoulder and face, having taken the full discharge of a shotgun blast as well as the single bullet. His body lay across the Louisville Slugger baseball bat he had been holding. Indications were emerging that a 'hit list' had been prepared and executed as the dead bodies were those of the bikie hierarchy. The shootings, although directed mostly at particular victims, also showed evidence of being indiscriminate. Near the entrance to the Tavern's lounge, a grim surprise was in store. Dressed in a pair of blue denim jeans and a striped, woollen jumper, lay the body of 14-year-old Leanne Walters. A large pool of blood had formed on the ground near her upper body.

Leanne was with the Rebels gang, another outlaw bikie gang who attended the swap meet and had seen her boyfriend in the firing line of the Bandidos. As she pushed him away, a .357 magnum bullet hit her in the face, removing the lower portion of her jaw. In an act of breathtaking bravery, she had taken the bullet meant for him.

'Jesus,' I said involuntarily. 'This isn't a bikie. Does anyone know her?'

'She's supposed to be the prize in our raffle,' came a well-juiced voice from behind me. 'Guess we'll have to refund all the ticket money now.'

'I'll fix you up later, arsehole,' was the response from a tall, bearded man with his long hair tied back in a ponytail. 'She's with us,' he said as he turned and faced me. 'She's not in any raffle.'

'What's your name?' I asked.

He looked at the ID card clipped to my coat pocket and said with resentment in his voice, 'Stretch, Mister Policeman. Why did those bastards bring their war here? Do you have to keep looking at her?'

I couldn't help it. Leanne had displayed the kind of courage that soldiers win medals for.

'Do you know who killed her, Stretch?' I asked him. 'No,' was his direct answer.

'Well you go and fix up "arsehole" and let me get on with finding her killer,' I replied, wondering if he would obey me.

He turned away and I saw that he wore the Colours of the Rebels: a red flag with crossed diagonal blue stripes carrying white stars. Another outlaw motorcycle gang was now the enemy of the Comanchero and Bandidos.

As I made my way back to the mobile command post, I looked down at my ID card with the red background, the insignia of an inspector. Dark blue was for sergeants and light blue for constables. Green was the colour for superintendents, and I had not seen any green cards on site. I was in charge of it all.

I sat in the director's chair and said to myself, 'Shit. What a mess.

Where do we go from here?'

I might have said a lot more if I had realised I was sitting near an unexploded bomb with enough power to obliterate everyone in the Tavern.

CHAPTER FOUR

The Arrests

The NSW Police and the general public can now reflect in hindsight and appreciate how fortunate we were that the massacre did not occur three years later. In 1984, the NSW Police Force was a large and united group of police officers, striving to uphold the ideal, 'Protection of Life and Property'. Our only boundaries were the interstate borders of New South Wales.

The Criminal Investigation Branch (CIB) formed part of the organisation, with a staff of about one thousand designated detectives, each working in specialist squads, performing duties for which they had been specifically trained. Homicide, Armed Hold-Up, Consorting, Breaking, Arson, Licensed Dealers, Motor and Scientific were some of the groups that were the matrix of the CIB.

As the officer-in-charge I had all of these squads from which to draw troops to supplement the small, overworked teams of detectives who represented a divisional contingent. The CIB was not confined to boundaries but was utilised state-wide to investigate serious and protracted inquiries.

The Sydney metropolitan NSW Police region was divided into 30 divisions. Milperra was in the Bankstown patrol of No. 19 Division. The detectives' strength of that division was 20 plainclothes officers led by a divisional detective sergeant. There was no way that such a group could properly investigate and manage a massacre of the proportion that occurred at Milperra. The obvious solution was to call in the CIB.

I summoned my five non-commissioned officers together to formulate a plan. The caravan was too small to hold all of us, so we stood outside. This was our first 'scrum down' or meeting.

I opened the meeting with an impromptu address: 'Let me speak, make your notes, absorb what I say and ask questions when I'm finished. Each of you has been given a task and he will know who I'm talking to as I go along. Okay?'

Each sergeant acknowledged this with a nod of his head. And this is what I told them:

- Separate the Bandidos and Comanchero and interview them in different lounges of the Tavern. Select teams of detectives, sufficient for two to each bikie. At least 100 detectives would be required.
- Take statements from all witnesses. If they can't be typed, record the information in the officer's notebook and have it signed by the deponent.
- Maintain isolation of the crime scene by uniformed officers. If the question of overtime arises, it will be authorised by the commander: me.
- Place an experienced detective in charge of the 'death squad'. The squad will attend to positive identification of the dead, accompany the corpses to the morgue and remain for the post-mortems.
- Visit injured persons at hospitals, and in the cases of suspects, arrange a police guard.
- Ascertain the locations of the Bandidos and Comanchero clubhouses, visit them and search for membership records and other documents or items of interest.
- All statements, documents and information, whether written or oral, must pass through the command post.

- Running sheets are to be given to the commander or his staff officer. They will nominate what further action is to be taken. Two female detectives are to collate those sheets. [Running sheets were used in serious crime investigations. Every piece of information was individually recorded on paper and signed by the submitting officer. The sheet was forwarded to the commander where, after careful reading it would be numbered, indexed and forwarded to an investigating detective for further attention. The running sheet was like a chain letter. If more inquiries were necessary, the running sheet was sent on to the next investigating officer. Woe betide anyone who broke this important chain. When finalised, the sheet might be as large as Tolstoy's *War and Peace* or it might have only one page. Whatever its size, it would be filed in a volume at the command post.]

- Have the crime scene photographed and then have the Photogrammetry Unit develop an accurate plan.

- The registration number of each vehicle at the Viking Tavern must be noted and placed on that plan.

- Have all weapons placed in the custody of an officer from the Ballistics Unit. An arsenal of shotguns, baseball bats, knives, chains, machetes and other weapons is to be assembled.

- Arrange and appoint a media officer to explain this debacle to the disbelieving public.

'That should start us off,' I said, pausing to catch my breath. 'Are there any questions?'

The crew answered as one, this time by shaking their heads. Whether it was done in acknowledgment or simply in amazement remained to be seen.

'Let's do it then,' I said as the scrum broke up.

Darryl Wilson got straight down to business and moved to a group of two dozen Bandidos huddled together on the Beaconsfield Street footpath. Undaunted, he stood before them and shouted, 'I am a police officer. Any of you men who were not involved in this brawl, please step forward.'

Not one person moved. That certainly helped identify some of the players.

Wilson was nicknamed 'Dapper'. A clean-cut cop, he was 40 years old and had experience as a crime scene examiner before transferring to the Homicide Squad. He possessed great nerve and courage, and to stand before 24 bikies and challenge their involvement in a fatal brawl fully tested those qualities.

I had learned from experience that when you are in charge of an operation, you relate to your officers what you want done but not how it should be done. Nothing saps the morale more than an officer telling you what he requires and then detailing how you should do the job. If Dapper wanted to confront the bikies, that was fine by me.

Aarne Tees moved in a different direction. With three detectives, he drove to the Comanchero clubhouse at 65 Harris Street, Harris Park, about 20 kilometres to the northwest of the Viking Tavern. It was a two-storey house and, on arrival, Tees found the place deserted.

Tees and his detectives broke open the front and rear doors without any opposition. The lower level of the house had been converted into a bar and poker machine area. Empty beer cans littered the floor and the smell of stale booze permeated the air.

A light switch was flicked on to reveal an unexpected surprise. Attached to a wall was a board with a number of photos of Bandidos bikies pinned to it. Across the picture of Bandidos Colin Campbell was written the word 'kill'. The board was actually a photographic hit list. A yellow cardboard folder nearby contained a copy of the Comanchero laws.

In an adjoining room – a lounge room – stood a wooden fixture with pegs attached, made up as a gun rack. Sitting in this contraption were a 12-gauge Smith and Wesson shotgun, a .22 calibre Squibman rifle, two pairs of karate sticks, a chain attached to a wooden handle, two Louisville Slugger baseball bats, ammunition for firearms and an ammunition belt. The gang's Regulations for Firearms were attached to the rack. Before he returned to Milperra, Aarne Tees set up a police guard at the clubhouse to await the arrival of a photographic team.

I had my own responsibilities to attend to, the first being to contact the reception officer (RO) at the CIB. This position was manned 24 hours every day and was occupied by a senior detective sergeant. All information relating to serious crimes or occurrences passed through the RO. He was the liaison officer to the police officer in the field, and would attend to every requirement.

I gave the RO a brief resume of what I knew to that time. The RO would then inform those who needed to know of what was occurring at Milperra. I needed the government medical officer or forensic pathologist at the scene. A body could be presumed to be deceased but never confirmed until examined by a doctor, especially a bikie's body, since it took a lot to kill them. The coroner should be informed as well.

A list of names flicked through my head as I reminded myself of the departmental adage: 'Let everyone know what has happened from the boss down to the cleaner'. I shortened the list and phoned Barney Ross, the Deputy Police Commissioner in charge of Operations, at his home.

Barney was an executive officer who had earned his rank through operational experience. He had served for many years as a ballistics expert and a crime scene examiner, attending the most macabre killings in this country. None, I thought as I spoke to him, as horrific as the spectacle before me.

Barney told me he would come out to the Viking Tavern. He was interested and wanted to support his officers. He had no ambitions of taking over but wanted to ensure that everything that was needed would be provided. The climb to the top had not dimmed his enthusiasm.

Next on my calling card was NSW Government Police Minister Peter Anderson. He was a former NSW Police officer and police prosecutor, and I found it easy to communicate with him in police jargon.

I finished my telephone calls and gazed out of the caravan door. I saw a lady dressed in another set of Colours, the uniform of the Salvation Army. She was standing next to a table at the outer perimeter of the crime scene. On the table was an urn of boiling water, polyurethane cups, tins of coffee and tea bags. An electric extension cord ran from the heater to an unseen power source, an infinitesimal distance away. Time for a coffee, straight black, no sugar, which I received with a friendly smile. The Salvos were always on hand, looking after both the good and the bad guys.

The statements, running sheets and verbal information flowed unremittingly from the officers in the field to the command post. From that information, I had to work out what was happening, make a judgment on what crimes had been committed and what prosecution, if any, should follow. That decision would have to be made soon. We could not hold the bikies without charging them with something. So far, we did not know who had committed the murders. The task of regrouping them for future interviews could prove impossible. Most of them would disappear, never to be seen again.

A Polair helicopter hovered overhead with a photographer on board, taking pictures from all angles of the crime scene. The Photogrammetry Unit were at work on the ground below, placing the 'witches' hats' at predetermined distances to enable an accurate plan of the scene to be produced. Land contours, distances, vehicles, buildings and shrubbery would all be included. Powerful arc lights were being set up to aid the police activities.

It was now approaching 11 pm and the bodies of the dead being removed from where they had been covered with sheets. The Bandidos and Comanchero were getting itchy. They resented being questioned by the police and were eager to leave. As I walked through the bar where the Bandidos were being interviewed, a bikie yelled, 'Arrest us or let us go'.

Don't tempt us, I thought. All in good time – our time.

I returned to the command post and called my leaders together and spoke to the five of them.

'Each member of the Comanchero and Bandidos has engaged in conduct that could cause terror to those people in the car park. The common law misdemeanour of affray would be an appropriate charge at this time.'

The team agreed. But nothing is ever simple, especially where the law is concerned.

'There is a hitch,' I continued. 'A common law misdemeanour can only be applied after the issue of a first instance warrant, which we do not have.' A first instance warrant is obtained from a magistrate after the police informant provides the magistrate with evidence on oath. 'However, if they are in custody, having been charged with another offence, the warrant is not necessary and the affray charge can be made. They should be charged with offensive behaviour, thus they could be in custody. Speak to your men and, if they are satisfied that their suspect might have committed this offence, we can proceed by charging first with offensive behaviour and then affray.'

The men left to confer with their teams. They each returned to the command post with a unanimous acceptance that a charge of offensive behaviour was the way to go.

The uniformed police who were at the Tavern had arrived by varying forms of transport, including a number of caged trucks. I located the drivers of seven of those vans and had them reverse their vehicles abreast and in line along one wall of the building next to the doors to the public bar.

Together with my officers, I entered the smoke-filled, crowded bar where the Bandidos and the detectives who had conducted interviews with them were waiting. In a voice that was hard to make heard, I announced, 'All you men have been placed under arrest. Take them to the trucks.'

Looks of disbelief spread across the bikies' faces and there were several groans of anger. But a quick glance about the room soon reminded them that they were outnumbered by police officers, and the police were armed.

The Bandidos were a sorry-looking lot after the long hours of interviews and the excitement of the battle had worn off. Bruising began to appear along with the accompanying aches and pains, fortified by the bad result of the melee. Their clothing reeked of cigarette smoke and the smell of body odour was overwhelming.

Two lines of lawmen formed a corridor leading from the entrance of the lounge to the police vans waiting with doors to the cages open. The Bandidos, some wearing bandages and dressings walked or limped to a van. When each van filled, the steel door was slammed closed, the safety bolt shot home and the padlock clipped shut. There were some shouts of abuse from within the cages, but the bikies had set the rules of this contest and were now reaping what they had sown. Three police vans accelerated out of the car park, blue lights flashing, heading to nearby Revesby Police Station.

I moved to the next bar, where the Comanchero had been taken. These bikies were also escorted to police vans. This time, however, the vans took their passengers to Bankstown Police Station. The two gangs had to be kept apart, especially when in custody.

The prevailing air of apprehension lifted from the Tavern with the removal of the two warring parties. Witnesses felt more at ease, as did many of the remaining police officers. Statements from witnesses to the crime had been taken and filled the correspondence boxes inside the mobile command post.

I watched the crime scene examiners working under the arc lights, knowing that their duties would take them through the night. They worked painstakingly and zealously, gathering every piece of evidence. Smaller items, such as firearms ammunition, spent and live, balls of shot and the cartridge shells from which they had been expelled were individually labelled and sealed in small plastic containers. Over 40 weapons had been recovered, labelled and safely placed in the custody of the Ballistics Unit.

A hand suddenly landed on my shoulder. With all the carnage around me, my nerves were already on edge and I jumped. I turned around quickly, ready to fight if necessary. But instead of a bikie, I found myself facing Barney Ross.

'Sorry, Ron,' he said, wryly amused by my fright. 'How's it going?' 'Slowly but surely, sir,' I replied honestly.

'I've been here a little while, but I stayed in the background. I didn't want to get in the way,' he said. 'Are you the senior man here? Are there no superintendents? Not that I think you're not capable, but you do need support.'

I told him that a couple of superintendents had attended the scene, but had since gone. I was the senior man and had been left with the ball to carry. With 30 years' operational experience behind me, I was confident that I could do the job.

CHAPTER FIVE

Let the Blood Dry

The seven bodies were examined where they fell by the coroner and the government pathologist. After this, the government contractors were called in to remove them. Each year, the NSW government called for tenders from the funeral industry to provide a service of removing corpses from the places where death had claimed them to a nominated mortuary. To the police, these people were simply called 'the contractors'.

Detective Sergeant Graham Lisle had been placed in charge of this distasteful segment of the investigation. He was a member of the Homicide Squad and was no stranger to the inside of a morgue. Graham Lisle had formed a team of seven uniformed police officers, one for each body. The deceased that were still to be positively identified would be viewed by relatives or friends on arrival at the city morgue. Identification in this instance was not straightforward because some of the deceased bikies were carrying fake IDs.

Identification of a body follows a pattern. A friend or relative identifies the corpse to a police officer who accompanies the body to a morgue. The officer 'books in' the deceased and enters brief details of how death was met into the morgue's admission book. The police officer then identifies the body formally to the forensic pathologist, who will decide whether or not a post-mortem examination will be conducted. He also makes an identification of the body to the coroner. This is a chain of events that never alters. It is as constant as death itself.

Graham Lisle and his squad followed the contractors' vehicles – station wagons with blacked-out windows – from Milperra to the city morgue at Glebe. The City Coroners' Courts are situated on Parramatta Road, opposite the grounds of the University of Sydney. The building is in a busy location on a main arterial highway connecting the City of Sydney to the City of Parramatta. The bustling world outside is a stark contrast to the quiet interior.

The police escort and their cargo passed the court building and drove to Arundel Street at the rear, a quiet street, so different from the highway one block removed. Not much traffic moved in this part of Arundel Street. Little wonder, as one of the building frontages was that of the city morgue.

The intercom system on the wall was activated, advising the morgue attendants of a delivery. The shutter door rose slowly and the two vehicles holding the bodies and the following police cars drove into a large, interior parking bay.

The attendants had been forewarned of a larger than normal admission and three men, dressed in baggy green jumpsuits, walked to the contractor's wagons. Dressed in large white rubber aprons and elbow-length rubber gloves, they removed the bodies and placed them on a stainless steel trolley.

There was little conversation between the men as the trolleys were wheeled to the dissecting room where ample tables existed on which each cadaver would be placed. Everything was made of stainless steel, even the doors to the chilling cabinets and the fluted tables which were fashioned to drain away the released body juices. Secured at the head of each table was a stainless steel tray holding the trepan or cutting tool, the countless probes and scalpels and a recording machine on which the pathologist would note the progress of his examination.

No surprise that conversation was limited. For several of the uniformed police officers, this was their first time inside a morgue, and the sightseeing was not recommended.

The chief forensic pathologist had returned from his visit to the crime scene. With the formalities of body identification having been completed at the morgue, he was ready to commence the autopsies. Present for that procedure were the uninitiated police officers and the more experienced members of the Scientific Branch who would witness the autopsies and obtain evidence of how each person had met their end.

Photographs were taken of each stage of the post-mortems. Shotgun pellets were removed from the bodies and the trajectories of bullet and stab wounds were noted. Bruising was now becoming more evident through the post-mortem staining with the stoppage of blood flow. Broken limbs showed the ferocity of the conflict.

The bodies had been stripped of their clothing, which was placed in separate plastic bags. The naked bodies looked surprisingly frail and vulnerable once their bikie Colours had been removed.

The officers from the Scientific Branch took copious notes of every minute detail of the examinations, from which they would prepare their statements of evidence to be given later at court. Some hours would pass before those inside that dreadful and perturbing examination room would escape and gratefully and greedily inhale the fresh, outside air. The smell of death is so acute, yet indescribable. It was common to see police standing motionless in the street outside a morgue, eagerly breathing in clean air.

A night had passed; a night of confusion, hard work and grief. I left the Viking Tavern at 5 am, the crime scene still isolated and maintained by police who had been there for 15 hours. As I drove towards Bankstown Police Station, thoughts rushed through my head of what lay ahead. Thirty-one Comanchero and Bandidos had been arrested, with others lying in hospital beds still to meet their nemesis. The two gangs had declared war against one another and their pitched battle had reverberated around the world, making headlines everywhere. Soon questions would be asked and answers demanded. Of me.

Bankstown Police Station was a typical suburban police station – a modestly built, square-shaped brick structure – used as the head station of the No. 19 Division police area. The station had recently acquired modern communication equipment, including a telex machine.

I sat beside the appliance and dictated to an operator all the information I had gathered concerning the bikie massacre. When typed and completed, the document was more than one metre in length. The transmission was sent to all senior executive officers of the department. No one could complain about being neglected, not even the cleaner.

At Bankstown Police Station, the Comanchero had been charged with offensive behaviour and affray. At the Revesby Station, the Bandidos had met a similar fate. Each bikie had been photographed, fingerprinted and all personal antecedents recorded. Identification had been secured and a form of control established. The bikies would appear before a magistrate at the Bankstown Court later that morning, when bail conditions would be discussed.

I made a telephone call to my home, letting my family know that it would still be some time before I would get away from work. A few things remained to be done.

I drove towards the city, stopping on the way for a Big Mac and a coffee at a Golden Arches outlet. The newspapers available to the customers were filled with pictures and reports of what had already been labelled the 'Milperra Massacre'. With my hunger satisfied, I hoped to satisfy any concerns my senior officers may have regarding the police response to the bikies' war.

The NSW Police Headquarters was situated in College Street, Sydney. As I stepped from the elevator on the twentieth level, I was ushered by a staff officer to the deputy chief's office. Barney Ross, Assistant Commissioner for Crime Bob Day and Bob Bradbury, the newly appointed chief of the CIB, were in conference. The Sydney daily newspapers were strewn across the floor and copies of my lengthy telex had been read by all three. But someone was missing. I looked around for the officer whom I would brief before handing over my command of the investigation. Where was he?

Barney must have read my mind. He calmly but firmly said, 'Ron, you have a handle on it. You started it, you finish it.'

I was stunned, yet also honoured. It is every cop's dream to head a major investigation. I would have to cancel my annual leave. I could not back down from the job. If a bikie war was breaking out, I wanted to do my best to end it. I decided to take it step by step, travel firmly and confidently, and select a number of men to form a team prepared to do the long journey.

I drove to the Bankstown local court, where the arrested bikies had been formally arraigned. Each bikie had been admitted to bail and they drifted away from the court, accompanied by their legal advocates.

The news media, both electronic and printed, surrounded me. Cameras, microphones and heads zoomed in on a face that had not seen a razor for over 24 hours, clothes that were crumpled and reeked of others' cigarette smoke, worn on a body that was beginning to tire. There was no make-up assistant for this performance. The probing questions began. 'Why isn't someone charged with murder?' 'What do you intend to do?' 'Why have they been allowed bail?'

I could only answer with that well-used police phrase, 'Inquiries are continuing'. This would be my mantra for the coming days.

A task force would have to be established to investigate the massacre and a suitable police station selected from which to operate. Most police stations in the Sydney metropolitan area had been fashioned from former houses with little interior space and limited outer grounds. These were unsuitable for a force of police who, apart from housing the number of personnel required, also needed space for parking a large fleet of cars.

Finally we chose Bass Hill Police Station, which was reasonably close to the scene of the crime and was situated in Marks Street, within the No. 19 Police Division. The station was modern and, since it had been built as a police station, catered well for police needs. It even had a large rear yard used as a holding yard for cars required as court exhibits.

Setting up a task force is not merely done by word of mouth. The three 'M's had to be considered – manpower, money and machinery. The officers were available, from the CIB, but the other two contingencies had to be considered.

A budget would be allocated from which wages, overtime witnesses, expenses, travelling, meals and other allowances plus the maintenance of motor vehicles would be drawn. The task of assessing and applying for these resources was mine to initiate. Just another job that came with the territory.

I returned to the crime scene at Milperra to find that the extensive police examination had been completed and could now be released from its confines. Motor vehicles began to move from the car park as witnesses reclaimed their property. The mobile command post moved out and headed towards its new home at Bass Hill.

In a space of minutes, what had earlier been a battleground, noisy and bullet-scarred, was now deserted. No one wanted to linger. Strips of chequered crime scene tape rustled in the wind. The blood of the victims, drying in the morning sun, marked where they had lain.

Years later, the bullet marks could still be seen around the hotel and car park. No one wanted to cover them up. They were part of Australian history.

CHAPTER SIX

The Brotherhood

A police investigation of an offence of this magnitude cannot commence without looking at the perpetrators and the reasons why they did it, but we didn't have a clue what we were dealing with. Until that September day, outlaw bikie gangs (OMGs) did not hold a very high profile in Australia. What the NSW Police Force did not understand was that we were standing toe-to-toe with a criminal network that was bigger, tougher and more powerful than the Mafia. The OMG were the most terrifying form of organisation we had faced and they were here, in Sydney.

I turned to the bikies' homeland, the United States, for help. The Federal Bureau of Investigation (FBI) and the US Justice Department had agents who were experts on OMGs and they informed me about bikies. Our raids on the Comanchero and Bandidos clubhouses had revealed interesting facts as well and, adding these to the FBI material, I was able to gain an understanding of the bikies' dark, esoteric world.

At the end of the Second World War, numbers of disgruntled servicemen found it difficult to return to civilian life. Many servicemen, back home in their own country and with common philosophies, a similar outlook on life and a mutual love of motorcycles, formed legitimate motorcycle clubs. Others, however, degenerated into disruptive and dangerous criminal groups more commonly referred to as OMGs.

Approximately one per cent of all citizens who owned and rode motorcycles fitted into this category and coined the phrase 'the one-per-centers'. A patch denoting this allegiance can be seen displayed on the various OMGs' Colours. Another patch, 'Our Colours Never Run', is also an indication of the wearer's attachment to his club.

Within the subculture of the OMGs is a display of pageantry that is both fascinating and repulsive. The bikies' Colours refer not only to the official club emblem but also to the leather or denim sleeveless jacket. The logo is usually positioned in the centre back of the jacket. Some gangs register a patent for their logo.

The patches worn on members' jackets have a specific meaning: 'MC' means the wearer is a member of a motorcycle gang, not a street gang; 'DFFL' means Dope Forever, Forever Loaded, a drug user; '13' signifies the thirteenth letter of the alphabet – M – indicating the wearer is a marijuana user; '1%' is an open statement that the wearer is a member of an OMG; 'Charter Member' indicates the wearer has been a member of his gang for at least five years; and 'Nomad' signifies an elite chapter of a gang with no geographical location.

The bikie culture is strictly hierarchical. Patches worn on the Colours denote the wearer's position in his gang: 'President', 'Sergeant at Arms', 'Vice President', 'Secretary' and 'Road Captain'. These were the bikies police should negotiate with during any confrontation as they hold power of veto within the gang.

OMGs each follow a similar structure and course of behaviour. Hells Angels were the first gang to appear as an OMG. At the conclusion of the Second World War, a group of war veterans formed a motorcycle club calling themselves the POBOBS (Pissed Off Bastards of Berdoo). The city of San Bernadino, east of Los

Angeles, had its name shortened to Berdoo and was where the gang originated.

In March 1948, the gang changed their name to Hells Angels and fashioned a grinning death's-head, wearing an old leather aviator's helmet with wings as their logo. The emblem was coloured red and white, and the Angels hold their Colours as sacred. In 1972, the gang received a patent from the US Patent Office.

Other gangs followed and, at the time of the Milperra Massacre there were eight hundred OMGs identified worldwide, ranging in size and sophistication from a single, loose-knit chapter to a multi-chapter enterprise. They adopted such intimidating gang names as Hells Angels, Black Uhlans, Outcasts, Nomads, Pagans, Gypsy Jokers, Fourth Reich, Rebels, Coffin Cheaters, Mob Shitters, Sadists, Phoenix, Lone Wolf, Gladiators, Renegades, Odin's Warriors, Outlaws and Finks to name a few, in addition to the Comanchero and Bandidos. The FBI in Washington documents criminal behaviour of some gangs with crimes such as murder, extortion, drug trafficking, kidnapping, witness intimidation, arson, prostitution, fraud and theft.

Before a bikie is accepted into an OMG as a 'Prospect', he must be introduced by a full member of the gang. An initiation ceremony may take place during which he is required to lie in the dirt while members urinate, defecate and vomit on him. His duties in the gang are menial and, on a club run, he will block off traffic at an intersection to allow his gang to pass through uninterrupted.

OMGs held three things in common: the love of their Colours, and an obsession with their motorcycle, and their women. Their motorcycles are usually Harley Davidsons in excess of 1100 cubic inch engine displacement. The machine is not only a means of transport but part of a bikie's mystique.

In many countries, the larger, well-established gangs owned their own motorcycle shops. The showrooms exhibited the latest in riding machines. The Dyna Wide Glide with its peach, black pearl, blue and grey colouring. The Softail, the Sportster and the Tourer, fitted with windshields, badland custom seats, black 'Live to Ride' handle grips, chrome slotted rear wheels, chrome forks and a full collection of medallions for fenders, grips, derby covers, mirrors and air filters.

The walls of the shops were plastered with colourful posters advertising the Harley. 'The Earth is Made of Stone and Chrome', 'On the World that is Your Harley Davidson', 'You Are the Creator and Life Has Just Begun', 'Live to Ride, Ride to Live', 'All These Years and the Road Hasn't Gotten Any Softer' and 'Move the Earth'.

The display cabinets and boards of genuine Harley parts filled the shops. Medallions, sissy bars, fuel tanks, bobtail fender racks, foot pegs, handlebars, short and long stem mirrors, speedometers, saddles all followed by the logos Fat Boy, Bad Boy, Hog, Hugger, Evolution, Electra Glide, Heritage, Softail, Ladies of Harleys, Springer, Low Rider and Screamin' Eagle.

All shops owned by the gangs were totally devoted to selling bikes.

Many were used for the disposal of stolen cycles and their parts.

The bikies referred to their women as their 'Real Ol' Ladies'. The women were allowed to wear a jacket with the bikie's gang name, but not the full Colours. 'Property of the (name of the gang)' was printed across the Ol' Lady's vest. Riding alongside her man, the Ol' Lady would often maintain a weapon or firearm, ready to arm her man in an emergency.

The women often obtained employment as topless waitresses in bikie-owned bars and nightspots and, with the permission of their bikie, would engage in prostitution. Many others were professional women and gained positions of trust and authority in security and intelligence industries, where they were capable of gaining sensitive information available for sale to the right buyer, with industrial espionage just one possibility.

They were also employed in government authorities, such as telephone companies, deliberately planted as neat, prim secretaries who used their positions to track down bikie enemies, many of whom had applied for unlisted phone numbers. And not once did one of those women betray the bikie gang she worked for.

The information that the FBI had gathered about these gangs showed a complex and global side to the war between the Bandidos and the Comanchero. The Bandidos regarded themselves worldwide as a nation and would not be intimidated by the smaller, Australian formation of the Comanchero.

When formed in 1966 as the Bandido Nation outlaw motorcycle gang in Houston, Texas, Donald Eugene Chambers was the founder and President. The name was changed to Bandidos before Chambers was convicted in the States during 1973 of two charges of murder. His position of President was then taken up by Ronald 'Ronnie' Jerome Hodge.

The Bandidos grew to an active membership that was sufficient to establish 28 chapters across the United States, with one elite chapter named the Nomads. This group was held responsible for internal discipline within the overall gangs of Bandidos, and they roamed the country keeping order.

Like the Mafia, the Bandidos operated amusement companies, topless bars, massage parlours and prostitution rackets, but their main source of wealth in the States was derived from the manufacture of amphetamines. With the introduction of the Bandidos into Sydney, the Americans had an Australian outlet in which to attempt the sale of their drugs. The new chapter was closely supervised by the headquarters in Texas.

Only nine months passed between the Comanchero's defection to the Bandidos and the war at Milperra. Surely there had been some indication to law enforcement agencies of the impending massacre?

The Bureau of Crime Intelligence (BCI) was a branch of the NSW Police Force created for the storing of crime-related information. Every incident or crime reported to police was acted upon, and a BCI form summarising the event was completed and forwarded to the bureau by the officer attending the occurrence.

The BCI was situated in the Remington Centre in Liverpool Street, Sydney, and occupied a complete level of that building. Hundreds of filing cabinets covered the floor space and contained sensitive documents relating to actual crimes as well as suspected ones.

I visited the centre and searched the files looking for all references to the two bikie gangs that may have forewarned us. Many confrontations between the two motorcycle gangs had taken place between December 1983 and September 1984. Shots had been fired into both gangs' clubhouses, members of both clubs had been seriously assaulted, stabbed and wounded by gunfire, run down in deliberate motor accidents and attacked when an invasion was made of the opposition's territory.

While both Comanchero and Bandidos had been injured, some seriously enough to require admission to hospital, the bikies' code of silence remained steadfast. No information was given to the police about the attacker: 'We will fix our own problem, we do not need the police', was the standard response.

The gathering and storing of information and intelligence serves no purpose unless it is acted upon. Reports received, stamped, indexed and filed without positive analysis proved nothing. The intelligence gained on the two bikie gangs should have warned us that more serious conflict was waiting to happen. But in 1984, such large-scale crimes were unheard of in Australia and no one really expected them.

As the result of my search at the BCI I learned that both Comanchero and Bandidos had similar characteristics, including:

- a strict code of silence throughout the membership of each gang

- disregard for law enforcement authority
- a practice of witness and law enforcement intimidation
- thrill seekers with ritualistic ceremonies
- use of sophisticated electronic equipment and
- counter-surveillance against law bodies and rival gangs.

Having completed my research on the OMG brotherhood, the next step in the investigation was to settle in to the Bass Hill base, select the staff and allocate their tasks.

CHAPTER SEVEN

The Bikie Task Force

The officer-in-charge of Bass Hill Police Station went on annual leave when 80 investigators and their possessions suddenly arrived at his normally quiet outpost. Like most police stations, Bass Hill catered for a diverse staff, general and uniformed duties police, detectives, highway patrol officers, licensing police, warrants and summons officers and those allocated to the charge room.

The charge room at Bass Hill was the reception area of the station. In command of all this was the station sergeant, seemingly chosen for that job because the only time he smiled was when he had wind. He was assisted in his duties by the reserve constable.

The detectives' room at the station consisted of a large office, with a smaller glassed-in room at one end where the detective in charge would supervise his officers. Extra desks and chairs were jammed into both rooms to accommodate the two 12-hour shifts of officers who would work continually, 24 hours each day, on the Milperra inquiry.

No investigation is complete without whiteboards, blackboards, any coloured board on which could be pinned photos of offenders, notices, crime scene photos, plans, all things of a visual nature that could assist the investigators in this massive inquiry.

Extra telephone lines so that each desk could have a phone, telex machines, cameras, stationery stores, car diaries, detectives' official diaries, a microwave oven and hot water urn. All were additional. A lecture room was part of the building, an ideal room for interviewing witnesses in private and for progress discussions (scrum downs) among the command staff.

Detectives who had searched the two gang clubhouses had obtained the clubs' membership records. They also observed that both premises had been fortified and were prepared for attack. Although the bikies' rules of war declared the homes and places of employment of the members as no-go zones, no such clemency was extended to the clubhouses.

Both gangs had boarded the windows of their clubhouses with tabletops. Old doors and planks of timber were secured across external doors. Savage dogs were placed on guard duty and rolls of barbed wire were stretched across entrances to their yards.

A gun parapet had been erected either side of the double gate to the rear yard of the Comanchero clubhouse. Armed 'Prospect' members performed sentry duties in the battlements to stave off any would-be intruder.

Two police officers trained in criminal analysis were assigned to the police contingent. These analysts would create charts on whiteboards, linking each bikie's connection to an event, his associates and history as an outlaw bikie. The charts enabled us to see at a glance the antecedents of each individual. Soon we were to know too well, the living and the dead.

A profile of each bikie was developed which included such details as name, aliases, date of birth, residential and workplace addresses, marital status, criminal history, motor vehicles owned and personal description, including tattoos. History of previous assaults and incidents committed by both gangs were added to the 'flow chart'. This gave the observer an immediate and clear picture of the association of all bikies involved in the war.

A police officer from the Public Relations Branch was assigned to help me with the number of press conferences I was required to attend. The whole world knew about the Milperra Massacre and the whole world wanted to know how the NSW Police would deal with it. The media machine had an endless appetite for the latest details of the investigation. The police PR officer would do his best to keep the media at bay, relieving me of any unnecessary interruption to the investigation.

Press conferences, however, were important. The public had a right to know of any progress we were making, and this information had to be delivered with caution and restraint. Misleading or damaging information could not be released as the legal representatives for the bikies would seize on it, record the data and later use it to discredit police witnesses at future court proceedings.

The large investigating team had to be given a name. It would simply be the 'Bikie Task Force'. And in order to complete the investigation, we would need the help of the Federal Bureau of Investigation.

The FBI liaison officer in Canberra was known by the euphemistic title of Attache to the Ambassador. He attended the task force office early in the inquiry and reintroduced himself to me. I remembered the first time I met him, several years before, while investigating a terrorist bomb attack on the Hakoah Club in Sydney.

At the entrance to the door of the US Embassy in Canberra, I had been confronted by two large, uniformed marines. After examining my credentials, I was escorted down several flights of stairs into the bowels of the building. There, I stood before a large fireproof door, similar to that of a bank vault, with a combination key lock in the centre. Within this soundproof, windowless, airconditioned room, I met the FBI agent. Our conversation was certainly held in private. Conditions were very different at Bass Hill in 1984, when he came calling on me.

He spoke slowly, deliberately and cautiously. 'Ron, this investigation has created intense interest in the States. I received a signal from home indicating Ronnie Hodge, the National Bandidos President and other senior bikies of the Nomad chapter attempted to come to Australia. Their visa applications were refused. They have sent four thousand dollars for floral arrangements at the funerals.'

Yes, the funerals, I was reminded. That raised another dilemma. Outlaw bikie gangs followed their own, unique proceedings when farewelling their departed brothers. Still vivid in my mind was a recent burial ceremony, eighteen months earlier, at the Palmdale Memorial Gardens on the state's central coast, where the Comanchero had purchased a number of burial sites for their fallen. A Comanchero had been killed during a long industrial dispute involving funeral directors. The bikies refused to wait for the strike to end and decided to bury their brother themselves. No one dared to accuse them of strike breaking. The coffin, attached to a Harley Davidson outfit and frame, minus the sidecar, was escorted from Sydney in bikie convoy to the cemetery, where President 'Jock' Ross, shouted to all present, 'No one tells the Comanchero when to bury their dead'. With rifles brought to the shoulders, a seven-gun salute broke the silence as the body of 'John Boy' was laid to rest. An unconfirmed police report stated that the melted down motorcycle of the deceased was buried with him.

It was highly probable that the two gangs, freshly armed with a new collection of firearms for the final salute to their fallen brothers, and their anger reignited, might well decide to celebrate the funeral wake with a further confrontation with their enemy. Just what we did not need, another bikie war. So we decided to act as peacekeepers at the funerals.

I sent Jim Counsel to the Comanchero clubhouse and Darryl Wilson to the Bandidos headquarters to deliver similar advice to both gangs. 'The war is over. Bury your dead with dignity and keep the wake peaceful. We will be there.'

Relatives of some of the deceased bikies had decided on private burials, which passed without incident. Other burials had a strong bikie, police and media presence, but the advice given to each group appeared to have been accepted and commonsense prevailed. Many hours passed afterwards at the ensuing wakes, where large quantities of consumed alcohol fuelled each gang's resentment of the other. A simmering air of apprehension existed. Following my initial 48 hours of uninterrupted duty, I settled into the pattern of working a 12-hour day, 7 am until 7 pm. The private hours at home were regularly infringed upon by staff reporting results of inquiries they considered I should be aware of: a blow-by-blow briefing. Then, as if by an afterthought, the reports were followed by a request for permission to work a bit of overtime. Times and conditions in the force had changed for the better since I was a young police officer. Overtime was now rightfully paid to officers needing to perform duties in excess hours of the rostered shift. I remembered only too well the long hours I had worked as a young detective, rewarded only by the knowledge of an investigation successfully concluded. All was done for the love of the job, certainly not for the money. But unfortunately I was a commissioned officer now and we were not included in the overtime allowance plan, only the NCOs qualified for it.

Sleep became difficult with thoughts, ideas and operational plans filling my mind. Each day, on arriving at Bass Hill to begin the day's activities, I would be briefed by the nightshift on what progress had been made during the previous 12 hours.

A daily meeting with my command team followed, when we would chew the cud and examine our options. We didn't have to strive for a breakthrough. This was an investigation with plain and obvious truths. Seven people had been killed at the hands of some forty people. But why? How did the normal bikie rivalry erupt into such lethal hatred? We knew who the players were, but the arduous task remained of piecing the deadly game together. Our morning meetings were productive and were irreverently referred to by the men as 'morning prayers'.

Our surveillance officers had observed that some bikies were conducting covert observations on us. Detectives leaving Bass Hill Station would be discreetly followed by bikies, not on their motorcycles but in cars. They wanted to find out where the investigators lived for 'future reference'. A sense of siege prevailed.

A room set aside at the police station took on the appearance of a miniature picture theatre. Copies of television film footage taken at the massacre had been obtained from the television channels and a group of detectives studied the recordings in an effort to identify all people appearing in the footage. Another team of police was then given the responsibility of locating those witnesses and obtaining their written statements.

Some motorcycle enthusiasts had their own personal cameras with them on the day of the shootings and had taken photographs while the massacre was happening. These films were developed and examined, and helped us to match up weapons with specific offenders.

The injured bikies who had been admitted to hospital were interviewed by task force investigators when their condition improved and doctors gave their approval. Upon their discharge, they too were charged with offensive behaviour and causing an affray. Forty offenders had been charged within seven days of Father's Day.

CHAPTER EIGHT

Common Purpose

The Chester Hill Pastry and Pie Shop was less than two kilometres from the task force headquarters. Police officers work odd hours and develop strange food preferences, but the meat pie is the staple of any diet. Eighty police had ensured that the pastry shop owner would increase his business beyond his wildest dreams.

Pastry cooks commence their work earlier than most police on a day shift, so by the time we had signed on and were ready to order breakfast, the pies were hot and waiting. A day of police duty inevitably commenced with a pie and sauce breakfast, washed down with a cup of coffee.

Within a fortnight, all Bandidos and Comanchero involved in the fatal conflict had been identified, or so we thought. We had compiled a list of 44 participants.

Like most small wars, this one was futile. The Presidents of both gangs who had ordered the war had survived and they, no doubt, had been prime targets in the battle. Jock Ross, President of the Comanchero, had shown a high visibility at the height of the battle while leading his Comanchero brothers into the fray. A spray of shotgun pellets had struck him in the head, with a metal fragment penetrating his skull. Miraculously, he had escaped death. Snoddy Spencer, the head of the Bandidos, had survived unscathed.

I sat down with my command team, accompanied by a senior police prosecutor, our legal brain Sergeant Frank McGoldrick. We had identified 43 suspects we knew had been in the battle. We knew that people had died, but we didn't know who had killed who. So what could we charge our bikies with? Our hope lay in common purpose.

The doctrine of common purpose was a proven, established legal principle that could be used to support a criminal charge in certain circumstances. The doctrine was simple. If two or more persons agreed to commit a particular crime, but in the process of committing that crime it went further and one of them committed another crime, all were responsible for the second crime. An accessory before the fact bears the same responsibility as the principal in the first degree. If it could be considered that the second crime could be contemplated as a possible incident of the planned offence, then the doctrine could be utilised. For example, if three offenders plan to commit an armed robbery at a bank and things go wrong in the bank and a bank employee is shot by one offender and killed, because that act came within the contemplation of what could happen, the three offenders could be charged and convicted of murder, supported by the doctrine of common purpose.

A clear indication had emerged from interviews with the bikies at the crime scene that it had been their intention to attend the Viking Tavern on 2 September 1984 armed with firearms and dangerous weapons, anticipating an armed confrontation with members of a rival bikie gang. Further, that if such a confrontation arose, they would inflict serious injury on one another. Jock's cry to his men of 'Kill 'em all' was proof of this. Therefore, it could be taken that if death resulted during the battle, everyone involved may each be responsible for that death. In this case, there were seven deaths.

A decision was made that an operation should be executed to arrest the 43 suspects, with a possibility, after interview, that a number of murder charges may follow. Every police operation is identified by a code name. This one would be 'Operation Hard Walk 84', the antonym of *Easy Rider*, a famous movie based on the bikie culture. Two hundred police officers from 30 metropolitan divisions would be involved in the operation.

A police operation does not just consist of police raiding homes of suspects, smashing down doors hoping to find someone to arrest. Procedures, directions, control and precautions have to be considered, recorded in writing and observed. The squad designated to prepare these orders would be Special Weapons Operation Squad (SWOS).

In 1945, a specialist unit was formed within the NSW Police Force as a section of the CIB. The group was called the Riot Squad and was created to deal with clashes between police and dangerous, armed criminals. The members of the squad received special training in the use of shotguns that was not available to other police officers.

The squad had two name changes, first to the Emergency Squad and later, in 1979, to the Special Weapons Operations Squad. A staff of 12 highly skilled officers were maintained as a permanent core. Their duties included training selected staff stationed throughout New South Wales to cope with local emergencies.

Before a police officer could qualify as a member of SWOS, he was required to be efficient in the use of:

- .38 calibre revolver
- .357 magnum revolver
- 12-gauge Remington 870 and Browning shotguns
- .223 calibre Colt, M16 rifle
- .223 calibre through to .309 calibre sniper rifles
- 9mm Uzi submachine gun
- chemical agents, and
- body armour.

A member of the squad could specialise in any number of areas, such as marksmanship, roping and rappelling, communication techniques, hostage negotiations, chemical weaponry, explosive ordinance recognition and disposal, witness protection procedures and high-speed elusive motor vehicle driving. Each officer was required to maintain a high standard of physical fitness by performing daily exercise. All SWOS operations were closely supervised by a senior officer qualified as a field commander.

SWOS officers dealt daily with emergency entries of buildings and always conformed to specially recognised operational orders called SMEAC, for Situation, Mission, Execution, Administration and logistics, Command and signals.

Paul McKinnon, a senior member of the squad, was an expert strategist who turned words into action with an alchemist's skill. He was directed to prepare the operational orders.

The date for Operation Hard Walk 84 was 21 September 1984. That day was a Friday and was chosen for a very good reason. Major criminal charges appeared to be more than a possibility against a number of offenders following the raids. Bail for the offenders would be opposed by the police because of the serious nature of the charges, the possibility of witness intimidation and the likelihood of some bikies absconding.

The defence lawyers in such a case would make immediate application to the Supreme Court for bail to be allowed and granted. This was also used by the defence to assess the strength or weakness of the prosecution's brief, as those details would be required to be given to the judge before a bail decision could be given. A Friday would at least give the police the opportunity of a weekend to prepare documents for court.

Police surveillance would now be intensified on the 43 targets to gain further knowledge of the bikies' intentions of future movement. The hunter had to think like his quarry. The bikies were aware of the existence of a police task force from their own observations and media coverage. The questions in their minds would be, were there any further charges to be laid? And if the answer was 'yes', should they stick around and wait for the axe to fall? Only the gang members knew that answer. The task force could only speculate on what was gained from surveillance reports.

The NSW Police Observation Squad was referred to in house as 'The Dogs'. Trained officers in the art of trailing and watching were used to record the behaviour and movements of suspects. The squad used a variety of disguise techniques to hide their police identity, usually whatever came to hand.

Strategies undertaken to disguise an officer could include setting up a road repair gang or a telephone line worker near a suspect's home. A council gardener in a nearby park or faking a car breakdown were other tactics, if circumstances permitted. When following a suspect vehicle at night, a specially fitted dipper switch in the Dog's car could cause a headlight to turn on or off or change the intensity of beam. The person being followed, when looking in the rear-vision mirror, would think that a different car was behind. Long-distance surveillance may be utilised and recorded in photography using cameras fitted with zoom lenses.

Police observations showed that the bikies were edgy and nervous, no doubt expecting further physical attacks from the opposing bikie gang. This posed a danger for the forthcoming Operation Hard Walk. Would the raiding police parties be mistaken for an attacking gang?

The bikies also showed a propensity for sleeping at each other's homes. The position could well arise during the planned police raids that more than one target may be found at a particular location. Every consideration was given to cover any contingency that could arise while preparing the SMEAC orders.

On Tuesday 18 September, Paul McKinnon handed me a six-page copy of the orders and said, 'See what you think about this. I'm sure I've covered everything.' The document was headed 'Operation Hard Walk 84':

SITUATION gave a general outline of the Viking Tavern massacre. Gang members of the Bandidos and Comanchero were listed together with their home addresses. Search warrants had been obtained for each. Simultaneous entry to all targets would be made.

MISSION in such orders is specified as a single action, with no double takes. Just one plain and simple objective: 'Arrest the offenders'. There could be no confusion in the operation. EXECUTION identified the police personnel of the 43 teams under my direction who would do the job at their target. Apart from any arrests, premises were to be searched for weapons, ammunition, explosives, drugs and apparatus for their manufacture, clothing and items signifying gang membership.

ADMINISTRATION and LOGISTICS identified the clothing to be worn by the raiding police, weapons they should carry and at what police station any arrested bikies should be charged.

COMMAND and SIGNALS explained that the operation would be conducted over the special Police Operations radio channel 3, and would commence at 4.30 am on 21 September 1984. Radio call signs were allocated to each team with portable radios being issued at an official pre-strike briefing. The Police Operations Centre would be at the Intelligence Branch building in Surry Hills, under my command. A list of other staff available for any emergency was provided. Entry to each targeted premises would be at 5 am on Friday 21 September 1984.

The operational orders were clearly defined and would leave the reader in no doubt about what was to be done. A three-page 'Coordinating Instruction' document accompanied the orders and would give each team leader full details regarding his personal target. In total there were 43 sets of these instructions, each varying in their evaluation of the team's objective.

Directions set out each target's code name, such as Sharks, Roosters, Bulldogs, Yellow, Orange and Alpha. The team leader and his group were listed and an assembly area given. Each team would be supplied with a similar document in reference to their target.

A suitable location had to be found to hold a briefing involving the two hundred plus police officers in order to plan the raids. Such a gathering of police would attract the news media like flies to a rubbish dump, thereby exposing our plans to the bikies. Bass Hill Police Station was under constant surveillance by both the media and bikie groups and, in any case, was too limited in space.

The SWOS underwent much of their training at the Holsworthy Army Camp to the south of Sydney, near Liverpool. The School of Military Engineering at the camp had an auditorium capable of housing the large briefing session. Police entering the complex would cause little excitement to the army personnel and the hall was some distance from the public roadway and well removed from the roving media eye. A touch of irony, I thought, because Comanchero Glen Eaves was a member of the army and had been attached to the base at the time of the massacre.

The SWOS staff had been working overtime to prepare the orders and instructions. The staff to be included in these documents had to be identified, selected and informed personally to be in attendance at Holsworthy by 2 pm on 20 September 1984.

Preference was given in the selection process to police officers with SWOS training in order that at least one such unit could be attached to each team and carry weapons unavailable to ordinary personnel. Dress was to be casual. The brains of a neurosurgeon were not required to infer that the bikies were the subject of this meeting.

Members of the Bikie Task Force from Bass Hill Station arrived at the army camp early on the morning of the briefing. Much preparation needed to be done to ensure the raids would be carried out competently and safely. Corkboards covered with individual photographs of members of each bikie gang were erected, with the criminal history of each man below his photo. There was also a large noticeboard dispaying information gained by law enforcement agencies overseas when they were searching outlaw bikies homes or clubhouses. The board stated in large letters:

WHAT TO LOOK FOR
Drugs • Weapons • Hidden compartments • Monies
Telephone numbers • Club constitution/by-laws Colours
• Meeting minutes • Stolen parts/property Fresh diggings
• Record books • Layouts and diagrams Membership
information • Mailing lists

WHAT TO EXPECT
Guard dogs • Video cameras • Burglar alarms Wife or Ol'
Lady • Various wild animals • Guards Scanners • Steel
doors • Intrusion devices Booby traps • Snakes • Snake
pits • Weapons Meshed windows • Sophisticated electronic
equipment

Forty-four bundles of papers had been compiled and labelled individually with the target codename. The packages were laid out on tables, one to each nominated team leader and contained the operational orders, coordinating instructions, search warrants, street maps relative to the location of the target, photo and personal history of the target, a brief resume of the bikie culture and what dangers could be expected.

Other display boards featured photographs of the crime scene and plans of the site, the Colours of the Bandidos and

Comanchero, club rules and the latest surveillance reports of the 43 targets.

At 2 pm on Thursday 20 September 1984, the doors to the auditorium were closed. Nobody would enter or exit the building until the briefing had been completed. Bob Day, the Assistant Commissioner (Crime) and Bob Bradbury, Chief of the CIB, sat alongside me on a raised platform at the head of the hall. Paul McKinnon stood at a lectern and opened the proceedings.

The chatter of two hundred police officers halted abruptly when McKinnon shouted, 'Attention! There will now be a rollcall. Remember there is an officer on parade.'

Each name was called and answered with a 'Sir' as the officer's presence was marked. McKinnon then delivered the operational orders in an authoritative manner, leaving nobody in doubt about the seriousness of the task that lay ahead. I then addressed the Hard Walk Team, urging them to keep the operation a total secret. Some police were in the habit of informing associates in the news media of pending police operations, not for any reward other than the possibility of getting their face on a television screen or in a newspaper.

'Do not leak this to the media. Their presence could abort an operation and lead to serious injury or death to those involved,' I stressed. My final words were taken from the popular TV American cop show *Hill Street Blues*, 'You be careful out there.'

With the briefing officially concluded, the groups began to assemble with their respective leaders to discuss the individual target they had been assigned. A critical time had arrived. The big picture had been outlined, now the finer details were discussed.

The expressions on the faces of the police officers were grim. They knew that at first light the following day, they were expected to make entry into 43 houses, occupied by armed bikies whose lives were devoted to breaking the law. The bikies could not be expected to give in without a fight. Slowly the men and women left the army base, sensing that the location had added a sense of proportion to the enormity of the task ahead.

Jim Brazel, the giant SWOS instructing officer, walked up to me and said, 'Good luck tomorrow, boss. This is a big one.'

He extended his hand and I could feel the casual power in his handshake. 'You too, Jim. I see you've taken on the Bandidos boss. Who's the doorman?' I asked.

'Me,' he replied matter-of-factly, as if house entry was the easiest job in the police force, not the most perilous.

Jim was born on the north coast at Macksville, on the Nambucca River. His father was a banana grower. Jim had worked as a shearer and, with his natural sporting ability, had soon won a contract to play rugby league football with the Glen Innes Club. In 1967, a severe drought forced him off the land and he moved to Sydney and joined the NSW Police Force. Jim was a fitness fanatic, training long and hard five days a week. He also worked as a fitness conditioner with a Sydney rugby league team.

Brazel had been a member of SWOS for over ten years and had been involved in three emergency entries a week during that period. I could visualise him at the front door of Snoddy Spencer's house, dressed in the SWOS black field uniform – black tunic and matching army-style pants with large pockets for any extra ammunition or small weapons that needed to be carried, black gaiters fastened around the ankle and extending onto heavy boots. A plain black, cotton cap completed the outfit. In his hands would be a Remington shotgun. No insignia of rank was displayed on the SWOS uniform, a lesson taken from the Native Americans. Don't indicate who the leader is. If he is taken out, the whole team may crumble.

Next to Brazel would be the keyman, nursing a sledgehammer in his arms, ready to take the door down with one blow. The doorman was the first into a building whether by forced entry or otherwise. The unknown of what lay beyond the door made the heart pump a little faster. Would it be an armed confrontation? A booby trap perhaps? Framed in a doorway, this officer was a sitting duck for anyone inside wanting to take him out. Seven people had already been murdered, would one more matter?

Braz was the doorman, and always in the back of his mind was the question every police officer asks himself: 'Would this be one door too many?'

CHAPTER NINE

The Raids

Pre-dawn, Friday 21 September 1984 and Operation Hard Walk was under way. Just three weeks had passed since the massacre, but all of those weeks, days and hours of devotion and decision were now to be put to the test.

I had spent a sleepless night, all the worries of the world seemed to descend during the time meant for rest. Had everything been covered? Did the bikies know what was happening? Had there been a leak to the press? Endless questions that would only be answered hopefully by day's end.

The command team assembled at 3.30 am in the Special Operations Room at the Intelligence Branch building in Campbell Street, Surry Hills. The building was the former home of the CIB, before it moved to the Remington Centre in Liverpool Street.

When occupied by detectives, the building was affectionately known as 'The Hat Factory'. In the old days, detectives were required to wear hats in order to properly salute their commissioned officers by doffing their headwear. Plainclothes police wore good hats for court attendance, not-so-good hats for day duties and old hats for night work. The Akubra hat factory was nearby and detectives purchased their hats there at cost price. Ironically, the police premises acquired a reputation of being a showroom for Akubra. Hence the nickname.

The operation room was brightly lit and filled with whiteboards, each containing written information relating to the 43 teams now on the road; banks of telephones with lists or emergency numbers alongside; a wireless operator's console; typewriters; telex machines; radio receivers and speakers; and a chair from which the commander would run this campaign.

I telephoned Central District Ambulance headquarters and a female voice answered. 'Can I speak to the supervisor?' I asked.

'My name is Mary. I am the switchgirl, the supervisor and whoever else you might want,' she said. The lady seemed quite friendly. I hoped I could trust her.

'This is Inspector Stephenson from the police. We have an operation taking place this morning which stretches across the Sydney metropolitan area. There may be injuries, so could you be alerted?' I asked.

'Certainly. What sort of injuries?' asked Mary.

'Gunshot,' I replied. 'Would you treat the information confidentially?'

'Of course,' she assured me.

A crucial item stood alone in a small kitchenette – the coffee machine. Cups of black coffee were taken by all in the room to settle the pre-combat adrenaline lift. No one was eating meat pies this morning.

At 4.30 am I gave the signal to Senior Constable Carter, the police radio or VKG operator, to commence Operation Hard Walk 84. He adjusted his headset and huffed into the microphone, 'Channel three now open.'

'Tango on,' came the first call. Followed by 'Bluebags on', 'Sharks on', until 43 teams had registered. A clear and simple message to me, letting me know the exact location of every officer involved in the operation. Not so clear, though, for the sleepless media hounds who monitor police radio channels for a worthwhile story. They would be frustrated in their attempts to work out what was going on.

At 5 am, entry time, concise messages came through as each team reported off at its location. 'Tigers off at target,' followed shortly with, 'Tigers back on with target.' Every officer involved understood what this jargon meant, where all personnel could be located with their prisoner. The police radio operator maintained a log of times, actions and results, which would continue until the conclusion of the operation.

The command team, although aware of the house entries, was deprived of the operational stimulus of being at the scene.

'Target Scarlet off,' came across the radio airwaves.

The six-man team of detectives, uniformed and Tactical Response Group officers had surrounded the weatherboard house at 993 Old Northern Road, Dural, a suburb to the northwest of Sydney.

Two detectives went to the front door, knocked loudly and called, 'Police here. We have a search warrant, open up.'

A curtain was pulled back slightly from a front window, followed by a shout from a female voice within, 'You'll have to go around the back.'

The two detectives moved cautiously to the rear of the house, leaving the other four officers to guard the front and side for any attempted escape. This was a well-used ploy by crooks: ask the police to go around to the back and then take off through the front door.

But on this occasion no ruse was involved. Once inside the house, police found that the front door had been securely locked and fastened with a piece of 4" by 2" timber nailed across the door jamb. A similar length of timber had been wedged against the door and nailed through the carpet into the floorboards.

'Bob' Watkin, the Bandidos occupant, stood armed with a .22 calibre rifle. Bob was taking no chances on an invasion from the Comanchero. The edict that no bikie should be attacked at his home had now been revoked. It was every man for himself.

Bob's home was searched, and although he was being taken into custody with the possibility of being charged with seven counts of murder, his main concern seemed to be the future care of his Colours that hung on the back of a lounge room chair. Satisfied that his Ol' Lady was an acceptable custodian of this jacket, the police and their target left.

'Scarlet back on with target,' sounded through the operation room.

Bob's Ol' Lady was quick to the telephone to alert other gang members of what had taken place. She was too late, however, the police had already hit.

'Target Carlton off,' echoed through the room as premises at Leich Avenue, Londonderry, in the western suburbs were searched by a four-man team of police. Then, 'Carlton back on without target.'

Not all the strikes were successful, but each team leader had been instructed to pursue all avenues of inquiry to locate his man. It was not surprising that Team Carlton continued to search for Comanchero Richard 'Chewey' Lorenz into the following day.

At 5.45 pm on Saturday 22 September 1984, the team returned to the Londonderry home after surveillance reported movement. Had the police arrived several minutes earlier, they would have been witnesses to the marriage of Chewey to his Ol' Lady, Kezra.

Chewey was aware of the police operation, but chose to get married rather than flee. Upon his arrest, he asked to spend five minutes of private time with his new bride. When the request was unromantically denied, he shrugged his shoulders and said, 'What's the difference? We may as well go.'

And go they did. With the bridegroom unlikely to return for some time, the bride was left with her wedding cake and guests.

'Target Alpha off,' came another report as the search for the giant 194-centimetre Bandido Anthony 'Tiny' Cain began. Tiny's home in the inner-city suburb of Birchgrove was deserted and, as news of the police operation received publicity, it was to prove extremely difficult to locate Tiny at his usual haunts. The 'Dogs', or surveillance officers, hit a brick wall. Cain did not want to join his bikie brothers in custody.

Almost a month passed before police got a break with Target Alpha. Members of the CIB Motor Squad attached to the Bikie Task Force were scanning one of Sydney's daily newspaper car sales pages when they noted a Ford sedan for sale, registration number ALQ164. The owner of this car was Tiny Cain. At 12.30 pm that day, an undercover police officer knocked on the door of 81 Crawford Road, Brighton le Sands, in Sydney's south. A giant of a man answered.

'I've come about the car for sale,' said the police officer.

'She's right there,' came the reply, with a nod of the head towards the white Ford parked in the street.

'Can we take her for a test drive?'

'Sure,' said Cain.

Tiny entered the passenger's side of the car with the undercover officer taking the driver's wheel. The vehicle was driven slowly along Crawford Road, but when it entered the first intersection, its progress was halted by a line of armed police officers stretched across the road.

'Struth!' said Tiny. 'I don't suppose you want to buy the car now?'

The major operation of Hard Walk 84 was closed down in the operations room by mid-morning on 21 September 1984. The final tally of the police action was 43 bikies arrested: 17 Comanchero and 26 Bandidos. Each man was charged with seven counts of murder – a total 301 counts of murder, an unprecedented number in criminal record history.

My mind flashed back to the crime scene. The first body I had encountered was Shadow Campbell being mourned by his real-life brother. Bull Campbell had now been arrested and charged with the murder of his brother. How ironic that charge seemed.

The day's duties continued for all officers involved in the operation: processing the offenders at the various police stations where the murder charges were laid; typing charge sheets for court; completing fingerprint forms and taking photographs for identification; sending telex messages to the senior district officers and headquarters; recording weapons and property seized during the arrests. The creation of a mountain of paperwork.

There was time for a quick cup of coffee and a meat pie, then off to court.

The prisoners were conveyed under police escort to local courts at Balmain, Bankstown, Blacktown, Burwood, Liverpool and Ryde. Never before had one person on his initial appearance before a magistrate been charged with so many counts of murder. The atmosphere at each court was electric. The secrecy of Hard Walk 84 had now been long eroded and the voracious reporters invaded the courts with their usual hunger for a headline-maker.

I returned to Bass Hill from the command post in the city to face a press conference comprised of city, country and interstate reporters. A brief, succinct synopsis of what had been achieved that morning was read out and the masses scurried to the phones to speak with their editors.

Police no longer required at court proceedings returned to Bass Hill. The Pie and Pastry Shop at Chester Hill would record 21 September 1984 as the golden day in the history of pie sales.

A debriefing had been timed for 1 pm that day at Task Force Command at Bass Hill. Team leaders no longer engaged in searches for their targets attended. Tired, grotty and nursing 'night-work belly', the dispositions were all surpassed by the one quality: success. No one had been injured during the operation – an amazing achievement considering the ferocity of the bikies involved.

News spreads quickly through the police force and is usually embellished as it passes from one person to another, making the final result quite different from the original. This news item, however, remained intact. There would be a social debriefing for the troops.

Bankstown Aero Club was a licensed social club and traded from an unpretentious clubhouse adjacent to Bankstown airport.

The club was in an out-of-the-way location, far away from the prying eyes of the media – somewhere to quietly relax after the hazards of the early morning operation.

As police completed their day's duty and signed off, they filtered into the club. They chatted about the highs and lows, hits and misses, the comical and depressing sides to their personal experiences. The apprehension from the preceding day's briefing had gone and the tension of the existing day was over.

Police Week had coincidentally been celebrated that day at the Bankstown Civic Centre, attended by NSW Police Commissioner John Avery and his deputy, Barney Ross. The unexpected appearance of the force's two top officers at the Aero Club to share the informal debriefing with their men instilled a sense of satisfaction in the team by the recognition of a difficult job well done by all.

The Commissioner placed a couple of notes on the bar and ordered a round of drinks for all. A toast was presented and accepted by the officers, drinking to the future of the NSW Police Force.

I returned home and, like so many of the Hard Walk officers, found it hard to unwind. The adrenaline was still pumping and the only way to settle it was to go out again. My family joined me at a local Chinese restaurant and, as we dined, I began to relax.

An aerial view of the Viking Tavern
car park. On 2 September 1984
there were approximately 200
vehicles and 500 people in the
car park.

Bandidos bikie gang Colours,
with the one-per-cent patch
clearly displayed

Comanchero bikie gang Colours.

TOP: The fighting continues at the Esso service station across the road from the Tavern after the police and ambulances have arrived. BOTTOM: The Bandidos business card.

TOP: Ambulance officers and police attending to the injured when the fighting ceased.

BOTTOM: The body of Comanchero Phillip Jeske, lying where he was shot.

TOP: Motorcycles lined up in the car park, some belonging to riders who would never return to collect them.
BOTTOM: Police officers hold back onlookers in Beaconsfield Street, outside the car park.

TOP: Three bodies in the car park, before transportation to the morgue.
BOTTOM: A lone Bandidos attracts the media as he leaves the Penrith courthouse, where his brothers await their fate.

A Comanchero vents his anger
at the press outside the courthouse,
unhappy with the outcome of
the trial.

CHAPTER TEN

The Bomb

The easiest part of operational policing is the arrest of an offender. Once the cell door slams shut behind him, the hard work of policing begins. We had to back up our charges with evidence. The bikies had money, enough money to hire a team of top defence lawyers. Those lawyers would use all their legal knowledge to oppose and prevent the admission of the police material; all part of the procedure to get their clients off the hook.

The weekend passed with the arresting police typing out summaries of the substance of their brief, preparing for the expected deluge of bail applications to the Supreme Court. Bail had been refused for each of the 43 bikies at the local courts and their lawyers were appealing.

On 25 September 1984, just four days after Operation Hard Walk, the arresting police were required to attend the Supreme Court, Sydney, in relation to bail applications by 11 of the defendants.

An overall résumé of the crime, followed by individual assessments of each applicant's involvement was given by police to Justice Carruthers. The following judgment was handed down:

It is a grave and awesome matter in our society to deprive a citizen of his liberty pending trial, particularly in a case

*such as the present where the delay between preferring the
charges and the trial must necessarily be substantial.*

*The legislation contemplates that circumstances may,
however, require such a deprivation of liberty to take place
and has specifically spelt out the relevant criteria which a
court is to take into consideration.*

*The circumstances of these alleged offences are
unprecedented in the social or criminal history of this
state. What happened on the afternoon of 2 September has
been appropriately described as a 'massacre' in an attempt
to depict the wholesale killing and wounding which took
place that afternoon.*

*I am satisfied in respect of each applicant, that the
Crown had and has available to it, evidence which fully
justified the arrest of each applicant and the preferring of
seven charges of murder.*

The bail applications were refused.

Justice Carruthers may have recalled a submission by a fellow
judge when assessing the character of a bikie. Justice Lazarus, at
the conclusion of a court case involving members of an OMG,
made the following observation:

*They dehumanise their members and those with whom
they associate: they enshrine sacrosanct rules and customs,
a code of conduct which is bestial, degrading and depraved
in the extreme. Their attitude towards women and girls
is at least vicious and despicable as that of any cult past or
present…*

The Bikie Task Force and Operation Hard Walk 84, although
focused on the same crime, were separate, independent creatures
with ongoing inquiries in their relative provinces. Another task

force was now established, its mission to prepare for the massive legal campaign that lay ahead.

Twelve senior non-commissioned officers were selected from the Bikie Task Force to form the Viking Task Force. I sat down with the new team and discussed my thoughts on how the prosecution case should proceed. To my mind, one joint hearing of the 43 bikies was the way to go. The task would be immense, but the alternative could prove calamitous.

A separate court determination, initially at the lower court and then at trial in the Supreme Court, would see witnesses recalled on 43 occasions to give their evidence. The charges would take an eternity to hear before a decision could be given, allowing for the willingness and availability of each witness to perpetually recount his or her evidence.

Further, evidence against one defendant might be rejected as inadmissible against another in separate hearings. The overall situation had to be disclosed with each defendant's participation and culpability revealed. After all, the doctrine of common purpose was being relied upon, so all defendants should appear in a common court hearing.

Naturally, the joint hearing procedure would be strenuously opposed by the defence. If the prosecution succeeded in their proposition, precedents would be set and milestones passed in areas quite apart from the formal recording of evidence.

My resolution for a massive, singular court hearing was supported by the problems experienced in a recent court case. Still vivid in my mind were the memories of the Bathurst Jail riot trials, where a number of prison inmates were charged with riotous behaviour causing damage to a jail in the mid-western district of New South Wales.

The offenders were brought to trial individually, causing a multiplicity of separate court proceedings that extended indefinitely. Police, prison officers and other witnesses and all associated with the inquiry were greatly inconvenienced by repeatedly presenting evidence before different panels of jurors. If dealt with in a similar manner, the Milperra Bikie Massacre hearing would throw the court system into turmoil for years, perhaps decades.

Doubt that such a singular hearing could be achieved arose even in the minds of some supporters, but the Viking Task Force remained steadfast in its resolve to have the evidence given in the one presentation. The police had laid the charges and it was now their responsibility to prove them in a manner deemed appropriate.

Any wavering commitment by some was soon dissipated when a letter was delivered to me at the Bass Hill centre. I pinned it to a noticeboard for all to see and read:

'Malong'
Boggabri 2382
26th September

Dear Detective Inspector Stephenson.

I meant to write this when the description of Hardwalk was first published, but I was travelling around Australia and writing seems difficult in such circumstances. Both my husband and I were enormously proud of the superb way you handled what must have been a pretty grim and nerve-racking assignment. Please accept our sincere congratulations to both your staff and yourself – your work must give most Australians a sense of safety.

Sincerely,
Elizabeth Moore

At least the public was on our side. And they were the ones who were paying us.

Approval was given to the NSW Police administration to be represented by counsel from the Office of the Director of Public Prosecutions at the forthcoming hearing. Mr Allan Viney, QC, and Peter Bodor, junior counsel, were briefed by solicitors Phillip Thompson and Peter Wood to lead the Crown case. Quite a twist of fate, I thought, as Allan Viney had appeared for the defence in the Bathurst Jail riot case and arduously and successfully opposed a singular hearing. Now he was being asked to change horses.

Application had been made by defence lawyers for the production of a number of informant-related witness statements. The appeal was resisted by the Crown. The court held that when statements were obtained by the police, they were done so on behalf of barristers who were heading the prosecution team. The statements were therefore privileged in so far as they were taken in a lawyer–client relationship.

The judgment was handed down by Justice Lusher, and the principles arising from that decision were to become an accepted legal authority or rule in future matters of a similar nature.

In order that a request could legitimately be made for a joint hearing, a suitable venue had to be found. A site in the Sydney metropolitan area was a prerequisite in order to be reasonably central to those witnesses required to give testimony. Transportation of the prisoners was also a concern. The 17 Comanchero were being held at the state penitentiary at Long Bay in the south of Sydney and the 26 Bandidos were at Parklea in the west.

I studied the State and Commonwealth government telephone directories for inspiration, but nothing jumped out at me. Next, I made contact with the executive of establishments such as Victoria Barracks Military Headquarters, military camps at Holsworthy and Ingleburn, Corrective Services prisons and all major courthouses. Nothing suitable was available.

The Hordern Pavilion, a building in the inner city used for large entertainment activities was considered and also rejected. Not only did the venue require ample space for the operation of a law court, but suitable custodial accommodation for 43 prisoners was a necessity. The bikies had been refused their bail applications and there was no reason to doubt that this situation would change. Where one building offered one aspect of adaptation, the other need was absent.

The Sydney City Coroner, Mr Gregory Glass, had been appointed to conduct the lower court committal proceedings and he had indicated a desire for an early start to the inquiry. The search for a suitable institution was urgent.

Police stations with adjoining courthouses were considered. The station would have to have cell accommodation large enough to contain 43 prisoners. All but one were unsuitable.

Penrith Police Station was at the western extremity of the Sydney metropolitan area, at the foot of the Blue Mountains. The station was large, modern and used as Police District Headquarters. An adjoining courthouse consisting of Supreme Court and local courtrooms formed part of the complex.

I met the Police Superintendent in Charge, Cliff McHardy, a former detective and friend of mine. Cliff showed me over the station, which contained a huge number of cells below ground, more than enough to hold the 43 bikies. Conference rooms were adjacent to the cells for lawyers to hold interviews with their clients. Above the cells, stairs led to the court complex consisting of five courtrooms used for summary and indictable judgments.

Courtroom No. 1, used as the Penrith District Court, was spacious but would require considerable structural alterations to contain the full cast of bikies, lawyers, cops and journalists. McHardy, surprisingly, accepted without protest the suggestion that his district should play host to all participants involved in the ensuing court proceedings. The burden of this decision would be enormous. Forty-three bikies, each in custody, were sure to attract to the district many more bikie supporters. An equal number of solicitors, barristers and QCs would be present, along with a prosecution team of six lawyers assisted by police prosecutors. The security measures and associated responsibilities were impossible to assess at that stage.

Police acceptance of the venue was only the initial step in the program. The structural alterations necessary to adapt the courtroom were beyond the province of the police authority. The courtroom was a dedicated area under the control of the

Chief Justice of New South Wales and the Department of the Attorney-General. Barney Ross made the necessary approaches on my behalf to those powers and gained their approval for alterations to be done.

The workmen from the State Public Works were not renowned for their speed or efficiency. Being involved to some degree with the bikie brief, however, brought out an urgency, a stimulation and dedication to their assignment. A six-man work gang met me at Penrith Courthouse and I found myself changing from a police officer to a work's foreman.

My directions were given verbally, no blueprints or plans were available. The prisoners' dock was only capable of holding six men, so other arrangements were necessary. The public gallery at the rear of the courtroom was to be enclosed with clear, shatterproof perspex and converted into a dock with separate divisions to secure the two bikie gangs. A sound system had to be installed in the converted dock to enable the defendants to hear all the evidence. The jury box had to be removed to accommodate the prosecution team, with the floor of the courtroom fully available to defence lawyers. The mezzanine public gallery would have to be improved to accommodate restricted members of the public, media and police.

These were just some of the requests put forward to the workers from the Properties Division of the Department of the Attorney-General. They were approved, so the men strapped on their equipment belts and went to work with crowbars, hammers, chisels, saws and electrical tools.

There was one final imposition: all work was to be completed in two weeks. The deadline of 23 October 1984 was the date set by the coroner to commence his hearing of the evidence. Not long for both sides – prosecution and defence – to prepare.

The robing rooms used by the legal fraternity would be fully occupied by the huge numbers of the defence personnel. Men and women in wigs and gowns had rules of etiquette and courtesy to follow. Places had to be found for the security of personal items as well as briefs of statements, law books and manuals.

Another problem was the legal apartheid which dictated that the prosecution lawyers could not mix with the defence lawyers. Where would the Crown assemblage be housed with their large brief of evidence, exhibits, communications equipment and all other privileges offered to the opposition?

The parking area at the rear of the police station and to the side of the courts provided ample space to accommodate a portable building, but it could not be installed at ground level as all vehicular access, including prisoner vans, to the station would be blocked. Steel pillars, 5 metres tall, would be installed on either side of the driveway and parking area, with a portable, four-roomed building to be lifted and settled on a platform, high above the ground. Two flights of steel staircases would provide access to the structure and, with air-conditioning units attached, the Crown would have a home. When it was completed, the building looked more like an ocean oil-drilling platform than a legal office.

The police also had building work to complete before the opening of court proceedings. Detective Sergeant Terry Baker was a long serving member of the NSW Scientific Branch. He was an expert at producing scale models of crime scenes. Terry had built a model of the Bathurst Jail used in a famous court case. He now accepted the tedious obligation of re-creating a 4 metre by 3 metre model of the Viking Tavern and the car park.

His work would be based on the plans and photographs taken at the crime scene. Plastic models of motorcycles and other vehicles would be fashioned, with registration numbers attached to each. The replicas would be fixed in the position in which they had been marked on the crime plan. Space had to be found in the courtroom, near the witness box, to enable witnesses to indicate where they were at the time of the killings.

Terry Baker would work tirelessly, day and night, to complete his model before the coroner began taking evidence. Once it was finished, we had to transport the elaborate model to the courthouse. Its installation meant filling more of the ever-decreasing available space.

All 43 bikies had been held in custody since their arrests on 21 September 1984. Their bail applications had been refused and the consequences of those decisions placed even more pressure on police planning and the resources available.

The bikies at Long Bay and Parklea were many kilometres from the Penrith court. I called on the service and expertise of Superintendent John Ure from Police Headquarters to assist me in preparing a system that would allow the rapid and safe transport of the prisoners to and from court daily. John was the officer-in-charge of security and crowd control measures when royalty or world dignitaries visited New South Wales, and his skills would be tested to the limit with this assignment.

Transportation and the security of the prisoners at Penrith Police Station meant the formation of yet another task force. I chose the codename Spartan, derived from Greek history and meaning 'dauntless, sternly disciplined and brave'. Such virtues would be required daily by the officers involved in this facet of the inquiry when dealing with hostile and vengeful bikies. Time restraints meant that the plan had to be completed and set in operation within two weeks.

The number of task forces was growing: Bikie, Hard Walk 84, Viking and now Spartan. Each had its own individual and unique purpose which, when combined, would ensure justice was done and the guilty punished. But is it ever as simple as that?

And then there was a horrible surprise. Towards the end of September, I was approached by a highway patrol officer named John Cook. He told me about the bomb.

'Boss, my name's Cook and I work on the highway patrol at Gosford on the bikes. I've formed a delicate relationship with some of the bikies because they do their runs through my patrol and I give them a bit of a go. A bikie who trusts me, so I'll only call him "Rabbit", wanted you to know that he knows about a bomb.'

'Tell me more,' I asked with a combination of dread and eagerness.

'He's gone to his sister's place at Maroochydore, but he's willing to meet you if I accompany you. He said it's got to do with Milperra,' he said.

Cook and I caught a plane packed with tourists up to Queensland's Sunshine Coast. But we weren't there to take in the sights. We were met at the airport by the local police, who had been forewarned of our arrival. Cookie left me at the police station, while he took a police car and picked up Rabbit and his sister, bringing them back to me.

Introductions were unnecessary as my visitors knew who I was. Rabbit was a bikie all right. Aged in his late thirties, six feet tall, full beard, long hair tied back in a ponytail and arms covered in tattoos. Even his face had tattooed teardrops under each eye. He was nervous and kept looking about him.

'It's okay. There's only you, your sister, John and I here. No one knows what this is all about,' I said to him reassuringly.

'I'll only tell you once and then I'm off. Don't bother looking for me again. I'm shit scared, but I want to unload before some poor bastard gets killed,' he said quietly.

'Okay, fair enough,' I said.

'On the day of the war, a Comanchero, an army bloke, took a few sticks of gelignite and a grenade to the pub. He was going to toss it at the Bandidos, but things got a bit hot so he shoved it into a ute. Did you find it?' he asked.

'No, we didn't,' I admitted, trying to hide my shock. 'Whose ute?' 'I don't know. Just some guy who was parked at the pub. If it's still there, the bloke's a walking time bomb,' he said.

'Will you give me a written statement? We might find the bomb, but we won't get how we found it into evidence without your help,' I asked, already knowing what his answer would be.

'No way. I've gone as far as I'm going.' 'Were you at Milperra?' I asked.

'No, but what I say is right. That's it, I've cleared myself,' were his final words to me.

Then he stood and, without a goodbye, he and his sister left the station and were driven away by Cook. I never met Rabbit again.

I telephoned Jim Counsel at Bass Hill and gave him the latest news. The Comanchero Rabbit had referred to had to be Glen Eaves, a member of the army, based in Sydney.

Jim examined a map of the crime scene and pinpointed Eaves's position from private photos taken during the action. He then noted the types of vehicles parked nearby and their registration numbers. One was a Holden utility. The owner had been a visitor at the swap meet in the car park on the day of the massacre, and was not associated with the Bandidos or Comanchero. He lived at Lidcombe. Jim met with a bomb appraisal specialist from the Scientific Branch and headed to that address.

Gelignite is a type of explosive that deteriorates quickly, losing its firmness to become a jelly-like substance. When the substance becomes loose and fluid, it also becomes very dangerous. In that state the smallest impact could cause it to explode, a detonation device was not necessary. We were looking for a bomb with devastating potential.

The owner of the ute wasn't at his home, but we learned that he worked not too far away at a factory in Villiers Road, Auburn. This time, the visit was successful. The utility was in the car park of the complex. Inquiries by police soon located the owner and he was told of the reason for the interest in his vehicle. The bomb expert was the only person to approach the utility. Dressed in protective clothing, he knelt at the rear of the vehicle and carefully and gently searched the spare wheel well of the ute. He withdrew a wet, soggy package which he carefully placed in a steel canister.

A Sydney newspaper, dated 1 September 1984, the day before the massacre, was wrapped around three sticks of gelignite with a length of fuse wire attached. Accompanying the explosive was an army simulator hand grenade. Rabbit's tip-off had saved many lives. No one was charged in relation to the bomb as the bikies had all been arrested during Operation Hard Walk and they could not be further interviewed.

Weapons of war had been taken to the Viking Tavern and indicated how purposeful and indiscriminate further killing would have been. A bomb and a hand grenade, thrown into a crowded car park containing five hundred people – the results did not bear considering. Our thanks went out to Rabbit for his display of conscience.

John Cook returned to the Maroochydore Police Station after parting company with Rabbit. A question was on my mind that I wanted to clear with the constable.

'John,' I asked, hoping for a credible answer. 'Why could Rabbit not have passed the information on to you? It would have saved a lot of bother.'

'It was all a matter of pride, boss. He didn't want to run to you or me, like a gig. He wanted us to run to him. I suppose, in his mind, that justified giving information to the police. He was making us work for it.'

CHAPTER ELEVEN

The Betrayal

At the time of the Milperra Massacre, Bernard Stephen Anthony Podgorski was 33 years old and lived in the western Sydney suburb of Glossodia. He was educated at St Patrick's College, Strathfield, where he gained his Higher School Certificate.

Married and the father of a four-month-old son, there was nothing in Bernie's life to indicate the infamy he would achieve.

Podgorski worked with the Hawkesbury Shire Council as a builder's assistant and in his spare time he played classical piano, golf and A-grade competition tennis. He was a dedicated family man, good to his wife and son and a good son himself to his parents. He was also a member of the Bandidos. Not just an ordinary member, but the gang's elected Secretary.

Podgorski was known to his bikie brothers by the gang name of Sheik. He had a reputation as a ladies' man and on bike runs would live in a tent, where he entertained his women. To his mind he was Valentino, The Sheik.

Bernie had been at Milperra, but escaped before the arrival of the police. A guilty conscience and uncertainty whether or not he was being sought by the police played on his mind. He had read and heard about the police arrests of Hard Walk 84 and wondered if he was on the wanted list. With a young family to care for, and a desire for self-preservation, he did not wish to finish in jail alongside his brothers. Sheik decided to look after himself. He telephoned the Bikie Task Force at Bass Hill and spoke to a detective.

'My name is Bernie Podgorski. I was a witness at Milperra. I might be able to help you.'

Podgorski told the detective that he was working on a building site at the Glossodia Community Hall and could be spoken to there. Greg Nomchong and Greg Bamford, both detective constables on the task force, were given the job of interviewing Bernie. Ironically, his name did not appear in any of the police records of persons either wanted for questioning as suspects or as a witness. The two detectives drove to the Glossodia building site in the stifling heat of a western Sydney spring day. On their arrival, Podgorski was located and taken to the foreman's office where he was interviewed. At first he denied being involved in the war at Milperra and asked if his name had been mentioned. The two young detectives could see that he was on a 'fishing expedition' to gain what knowledge, if any, the police had to involve him.

Bernie was heavily tattooed on his arms, one in particular attracted the attention of the two police officers. They both saw it at the same time and looked at each other. 'BFFB': Bandidos Forever, Forever Bandidos.

Bernie's bikie identity was quickly revealed. After being cautioned, he admitted that he had participated in the massacre. He did not carry a firearm, only a baseball bat, and he did not kill anyone. At least that was his story. Bernie had been at the crime scene and had assisted his Bandidos brothers, which was enough to arrest him.

There is an old saying among detectives, 'The brief can only get better'. Bernie was about to make bikie history. He wanted to do a deal. For the first time ever, a bikie decided to roll over and squeal. It was an act that reverberated throughout the bikie world. The bikies' strict code of silence was to be broken by the third most senior member of Bandidos Australia. The penalty would not have to be debated by his brothers, it was laid down in the rules. Bernie's future would be a death sentence, the bikies' version of a fatwa.

Podgorski was brought to Bass Hill, where I spoke with him. 'I understand that you want out?' I probed.

'I want to speak to my solicitor first,' he replied, giving nothing away.

I contacted Frank Hoare, who was Podgorski's legal adviser, as requested. Frank arrived at Bass Hill within the hour.

Sheik was six feet tall, well proportioned, with long brown hair pulled back and tied in a ponytail. His arms were covered in tattoos, but otherwise he looked like any other labourer. He was dirty, but then he was in his work clothes and had just been taken off a work site.

Jim Counsel was my confidant and I advised him of this sudden act of providence. I wanted Jim to take charge of the Bandidos Secretary. The charges against each bikie were justifiable and strong, but there was no doubt that Podgorski's testimony could be the linchpin, a corroboration of the police evidence from the enemy's camp.

Two days remained before the opening bat would be called to give evidence before Coroner Greg Glass. Sheik and his lawyer had been allowed to speak privately for over an hour before I sat down with them, Jim Counsel and Greg Bamford.

I opened the meeting with the question, 'What do you wish to say, Mr Hoare?'

'My client is asking for immunity,' was the simple request.

'I can't give immunity. That's a matter for the Attorney-General,' I said quite honestly. 'And I want you to understand that we do not need his help. Because he was present, Bernie will be charged with seven counts of murder at the Viking Tavern on Father's Day.'

'I understand,' said Hoare. 'What do we have to do?'

'Detective Counsel will act as Bernie's case officer. We will record an interview with your client. I stress that we do not need this information. It is a decision you must make. I can only forward your request for immunity to the Attorney-General.'

Both Sheik and his solicitor understood.

Podgorski's confession was 23 pages long and it read like a script for a *Mad Max* movie. It also unlocked the secrets of the Milperra Massacre.

Sheik was originally a member of Loners Motorcycle Club, a small outlaw bikie club, which disbanded after the members were assaulted by Jock and his Comanchero. The Loners were coerced into joining Jock's gang and Podgorski described how that 'merger' took place:

> One of our blokes was at the Milton Hotel and his mate was king-hit by one of the Comanchero. The member of the Loners returned to the Milton Hotel with a shotgun and threatened several Comanchero.
>
> They hit our clubhouse at 143 Palmer Street, Sydney. They assaulted three of our members who were living there with baseball bats and put them in St Vincent's Hospital for seven or eight days.
>
> Later, we were contacted by the Comanchero for a friendly meeting at the Milton Hotel, but when we arrived, cars surrounded us from side streets, blokes jumped out of cars and started bashing us with baseball bats and iron bars. A number of shots were fired at us. There was about twenty of them. If you can't beat them, join them.

Sheik went on to become a full member of the Comanchero until 1983, when he joined a breakaway group to become a foundation member of the Sydney chapter of the Bandidos. He described the rift in the Comanchero being caused by Jock Ross after he declared himself Supreme Commander with total power, overruling the previously accepted voting system.

Jock was strict. 'No heroin was allowed in the club at all,' said Podgorski. 'Nobody was allowed to play up with anybody else's missus. They would be bashed and thrown out of the club. If there was a fight and you didn't back up your brother, you would be thrown out of the club.'

Podgorski then related a rule that would support our doctrine of common purpose: 'For the club to go to war with another club, a unanimous vote is required. One in, all in.'

The Comanchero gang had been depleted to only 12 members when the other members defected. The final insult came when the premises in Louisa Street, Birchgrove, originally the Comanchero clubhouse, was taken over by the Bandidos. The Comanchero were forced to re-establish themselves at their present address in Harris Park.

There were a number of bashings. During July 1984, a lone Bandidos was assaulted by a number of Comanchero while attending a motorcycle swap meet. He received a broken jaw and a stab wound to the neck. This started a reaction by the Bandidos, who grouped and then ventured into Comanchero territory at the Bull and Bush Hotel at Baulkham Hills. Three Comanchero were badly beaten.

Later, shots were fired from a shotgun into the Bandidos clubhouse by two Comanchero who were later killed in the Father's Day Massacre. Milperra, apart from being a war, was also an opportunity for revenge.

Outlaw bikie gangs are very territorial and any intrusion into a gang's patch by an unauthorised group is condemned. Fights occurred at the Royal Oak Hotel at Parramatta, which was described as a Bandidos hotel – territory from which Comanchero were banned.

Other territorial disputes arose and prompted further assaults between the two gangs. The incidents became more frequent and, if possible, more violent. In August 1984, Jock Ross was shunted off his Harley Davidson and pushed 65 metres along a roadway by a Bandidos in a one-tonne truck.

On three further occasions, shots were exchanged by the opposing gangs and it became acutely evident that their differences would never be settled peacefully. Podgorski described a meeting in July 1984 at the Bandidos clubhouse where the members were addressed by their President, Snoddy Spencer.

'Something has got to be done about Jock and the Comanchero. Anyone in the club who has got any guts and wants to get rid of the problem, not just bashing them, meet me in the bar after the meeting. We need to fix Jock permanently.'

Snoddy's statement was clear and specific to all. Jock had to go, and any Comanchero who supported him would go as well. A declaration of war against the Comanchero was voted on and passed.

Bikies from both gangs began to arm themselves. No bikie would venture out onto the road without a weapon on his body or his machine. Snoddy armed himself with two firearms, one a Smith and Wesson shotgun and the other a Rossi .357 magnum. Bullets from the Rossi struck and killed Leanne Walters as well as the two Comanchero Foghorn Lane and Leroy Jeske at the Viking Tavern.

Bandidos Tiny Cain bought three 12-gauge shotguns, which were also used at the Viking Tavern. One of the weapons was purchased by the gang as a prize in a raffle.

Podgorski commented on the security arrangements that were put in place at the clubhouse:

We obtained a half shepherd cross dog to warn if anybody was coming. The nominees were put on a roster shift at night-times and daytimes around the clubhouse. An assortment of baseball bats and other implements put around the doors and windows, and bottles and so forth.

The club had a pump-action shotgun – the nominees
would have that with them when they were on duty.

The Comanchero were not left idle in their preparation for the expected war. Foghorn Lane had purchased a CB radio which was used to communicate with their gang members carrying two-way radios during the Viking battle. Police had located the radio in Glen Eaves's car after the massacre.

Ivan Romceck purchased a 12-gauge Bentley shotgun, which was later taken into possession by the police at the scene of the massacre. The shotgun had been discharged and spent shells from the weapon were found in the car park.

Podgorski, as Secretary for the Bandidos, had recorded the making of the war declaration and other decisions in a thick red book labelled 'Minutes of Meeting'. That book held information of major importance. The damaging entries could be attested to by the author and admitted into evidence. But where was the book? It had not been found by the police who searched the Bandidos clubhouse. A written description of the gang's intentions would corroborate all that Podgorski was relating. He could not be accused of lying.

Two nights before the massacre, the Bandidos met at their clubhouse. A bikie swap meeting had been advertised through the biker world to take place on Father's Day in the car park of the Viking Tavern at Milperra. A scout would be sent from the Bandidos on that day to find out if the Comanchero were present. If they were, the Viking Tavern would be the battlefield.

The club bar opened and the beer flowed. The smell of conflict and victory flared the nostrils of the Bandidos. Targets were discussed and allocations of who should 'hit' who were handed down by Snoddy. His accompanying instructions were, 'They're to be bashed and done and their Colours taken.'

Sheik then described the events of 2 September 1984:

I left home about eight o'clock in the morning from my
home at Glossodia. I celebrated Father's Day with my
family and had lunch with them at their home. Later
I went to Lance Wellington's home at Pringle Avenue,
Bankstown – the members of the club were in ones and
twos – a few of the members had earlier ridden past Glen
Eaves's home to stir him up and make sure he would be at
the Tavern.

Caesar said to me, 'You're a rover.' I asked, 'What do I
do?'

He just said, 'Certain blokes have certain targets and
the rovers are to bash anyone that is getting on top of our
blokes.'

We left for the Viking Tavern. Bull was driving his
Holden and Chopper was in the passenger's seat, Whack
and Roach were in the back. I went in the Falcon with
Shadow, Lard, Lout, Tiny and Bear. Then the bikes came
out. Davo was on his trike, Lance on his sidecar with one
on the back. Then there was Tony and Rua, Hookey, Zorba
and Luey. Caesar was on his own bike, then Kid Rotten and
Opey. We travelled towards the Viking in formation.

A bikie formation was how a gang lined up for a run. This was a
special run. The President would ride at the front, followed by
the full Colour members. The Sergeant at Arms would ride in the
last row of the regular members, ahead of the Prospect members.
At the rear came the war wagon, which usually carried beer and
camping equipment. On this occasion, the cargo was weapons.
Podgorski continued:

The bikes pulled up and the members got off. We walked
briskly towards the Comanchero. I was standing to the
left of Zorba; there were five or six Comanchero facing us
with guns. There was Leroy with a shotgun, Eaves and also

Sparrow. Zorba went to grab the shotgun that Eaves was
carrying and it discharged. Then I saw Sparrow hit Zorba
over the head with a club. Zorba wrestled Sparrow down
and a girl came and hit Zorba over the head with a baseball
bat.
  Guns went off and I hit the ground. I could see Jock.
He had a machete in his hand and was waving it above his
head and shouting, 'Kill 'em all'.
  There were bodies on the ground, brothers dead.

Bernie Podgorski was not only a member of the Bandidos but
also a former Comanchero. He knew most of the members on
both sides of this war. A little further questioning and the whole
scenario of the battlefield would be coaxed from him.

Glen Eaves's car was parked in the car park near the Tavern
building and a number of Comanchero were gathered alongside
waiting for the Bandidos to arrive. Eaves was armed with a shotgun
and Ivan Romcek, who was later killed in the battle, stood by with
another shotgun.

Sunshine Kucler, also armed with a shotgun, was standing near
the entrance to the Lounge Bar, holding his weapon ready to fire.
Two other Comanchero, Tony McCoy and Robert Lane, stood
near the entrance to the public bar. The other gang members
were scattered through the five hundred people in the car park.

'They were waiting for us,' said Podgorski. 'All the gang. I could
see Jock out in the middle with his hair parter.' Sheik went on to
tell what happened when he arrived with the Bandidos.

Snoddy left his car, which he had parked close to Glen
Eaves. He lent over the hood, aiming his Rossi .357 rifle at the
Comanchero. The remaining Bandidos left their transport and
walked in a line through the car park yelling abuse and screaming
at the Comanchero.

Podgorski didn't know who fired the first shot but when it
happened, 'all hell broke loose'.

Snoddy was active with his rifle, accounting for three victims: Phillip Jeske, Robert Lane and the young girl, Leanne Walters.

'I shit myself and hit the ground. Jock was near me, screaming out. He was off his head,' said Bernie. 'Shots were going off. It's a wonder there weren't more killed. The cops got there pretty quick. I wasn't going to hang around.'

Sheik knew that his Colours would give him away. He dropped the iron bar he was armed with, removed his jacket with the Bandidos emblem, folded it over and shoved it up under his arm. He then simply walked away in the turmoil that surrounded him. From what Podgorski had related, there was little doubt that a hit list of the Comanchero hierarchy had been decided upon and anyone else who suffered would be just bad luck. With the war having been declared, the members of both gangs took part, under the direct orders of their President.

As Podgorski related his revelation, Jim Counsel typed and recorded all that was said. I thought of the parallels that existed between the bikies and the police. Like them, we had our rules. Sheik had disclosed some gang names. We too had nicknames in our task force: Dasher, Spy, Midnight, Rughead, Tip. We also had our Colours: the blue-and-white chequered hatband and the rank of the office bearers were clearly displayed in the chevrons on the arms, and crowns and stars on the shoulders. But that was where the similarities ceased. Our two cultures were poles apart, the bikies were the 'one-per-centers', the outlaws. The police, the 99-per-centers, were lawmen and women.

Sheik was charged with seven counts of murder, his fate at this time similar to that of his brothers. He was not yet immune from legal action, but he would never be free of his punishment from the one-per-centers. His betrayal would haunt him as long as he lived. He would be known throughout the bikie world as 'Dead Meat' Podgorski.

He was denied bail by the police, which was what he wanted. To be free and at large would expose him to danger. Not only had he betrayed the Comanchero and Bandidos, but the entire outlaw bikie family.

According to the FBI manual, the Outlaws, one of the major outlaw motorcycle gangs, held a philosophy that was universally adopted by other gangs. It is summarised by a motto, 'God Forgives – Bikies Don't'.

Their creed was strict. It left little doubt about Sheik's future.

A one-per-center is the one of a hundred of us who have given up on society and the politicians' one which was law. This is why we look repulsive. We are saying, 'We don't want to be like you, to look like you, so Stay Out of Our Face. Look at your Brother standing next to you and ask yourself if you would give him half of what you have in your pocket, or half of what you have to eat. If a citizen hits your Brother, will you be on him without asking why? There is no why. Your Brother isn't always right, but he is always your Brother. It's one in all and all in one. If you don't think that way then walk away, because you are a citizen and don't belong with us. We are outlaws and will follow our way. All members are your Brothers and your family. You will not steal your Brother's possessions, money, woman, class or his humour. If you do this, your Brother will do you.'

Bernie Podgorski had broken the bikies' rules. He had rolled over. No other outlaw was ever before known to have ratted. Sheik was now a police informer and, whatever side you supported, *informant* was a dirty word meaning betrayer, squealer, traitor, a Judas. His testimony would support the brief enormously, but to me, any form of betrayal to a cause could only be received with revulsion.

The safety of Sheik became the responsibility of the Bikie Task Force. We knew if he was sent to a remand prison there would be some hit men after him within hours of his arrival. We needed him alive.

I spoke to Jim Counsel. 'You're going have to live with this bloke and look after him until a decision has been made by the Attorney-General on whether or not he will give him immunity. He's in our custody, bail has been refused, so I want you to take him to Springwood Police Station where he will have a cell to himself. But you'll have to stick with him until a decision is made.'

I knew it was a big ask. Jim was married with a family, but now he would have to spend both his work and leisure time with Sheik. Jim left Bass Hill with Podgorski in handcuffs, and travelled west to the Blue Mountains, where both men would live in isolation until the Attorney-General delivered a result.

Frank Hoare submitted his written entreaty and handed it to me saying, 'He's done the right thing. I hope you look after him.'

'We'll do our best,' I said. Sheik should have thought of the consequences before he willingly became involved in the war.

I added a lengthy appraisal to the application, citing the value of Sheik's evidence to the overall brief. Then I sent the document to Allan Viney, QC. He would add the final words to the document on which the NSW Attorney-General would make his decision.

On 30 October 1984, Bernard Podgorski was granted immunity from prosecution to murder on condition that he reveal all he knew about the Milperra Massacre. The Bandidos Secretary would now be freed from police custody in one sense, but recommitted in another. He would enter the Witness Protection Program. He would be a marked man for all his life.

CHAPTER TWELVE

The Minders

In 1984 the Witness Protection Unit of the NSW Police Force was in its infancy. In fact, Podgorski would be its first client. We had chosen a hell of a way to begin. Sheik was being hunted by the most dangerous underworld hit men on the planet. The entire bikie brotherhood wanted him dead.

The unit was a segment of the Special Weapons Operations Squad and two sergeants were responsible for its formation and operation. They were Jim Brazel, nicknamed Cougar because of his piercing brown eyes and amazing agility, and John O'Neill. John was known as 'Boom Boom'. He was short and solidly built, but nothing about his appearance explained why he earned this sobriquet, so I asked him.

'When I started in plainclothes, I was stationed at Waverley. The boss there was a sergeant named Gordon Beardmore and he said to me, "Jesus, you're the shortest detective I've ever seen. I want big cannons here, but they've sent you to me. I'll just have to call you Boom Boom, the little cannon,"' he explained.

Officers from the Tactical Response Group and female police officers formed the nucleus of the unit that would protect Sheik. A total of 20 police in all would be necessary, full-time, to see him through his court appearances, which were expected to last for two years.

These officers were specially selected for their ability to perform under stress. Protecting a witness was not just about keeping him or her out of sight. When in the public view, the witness had to be physically shielded by four officers in what was called 'close body protection formation'.

Long and lonely hours of isolation, such as those experienced by the protected witness, would also be shared by the minders. Night-time vigils caused a lot of apprehension. Special night glasses would be worn by outside watchers or guards.

Apart from Podgorski, his wife, baby son and the family's German shepherd also came within the protection program. The dog would cause as much inconvenience as its owners, but was later described by one member of the unit as 'the best of the bunch'. The animal had to be exercised and, at times, boarded in a registered kennel.

A 'safe house' had to be selected, and the first one chosen was the NSW Police Academy at Goulburn. The campus was large and made up of a number of buildings used for the accommodation of the police trainees. The buildings were called tower blocks. A complete block was set aside for the Podgorskis.

John O'Neill met Jim Counsel at Springwood Police Station and relieved Jim of the care of Sheik. An American President would have had as much security. A contingent of 20 officers was required, using five motor vehicles. A scout car would set out first at the head of the convoy. This car would drive ahead and take observations, before dropping back to cover the rear of the fleet. Then came the lead car, followed by the principal car containing Sheik, John O'Neill and three other officers. A tail car and point car made up the procession. Officers in each car were armed with submachine guns, and Podgorski remarked, 'That's good, because our blokes have got those too.'

When the escort travelled from Goulburn to the Penrith court, it would be by way of the Western Motorway as the fast lanes were considered the safe lanes. When the escort entered the Sydney metropolitan area, the scout car would halt traffic at control lights and direct the convoy through unimpeded. An uninterrupted journey was essential. A stationary witness made an easier target.

At other times, when Sheik had to be taken into the city for conferences, a request was made to the Brisbane Street traffic control centre for a 'green light route'. The convoy's progress was monitored through cameras and green lights were given at all intersections. This was a system used when VIPs were travelling through Sydney to the international airport at Mascot. It was for celebrities, and Sheik was certainly a celebrity.

Special arrangements were made through two state government departments to alter the the Podgorskis' identities. The Department of Motor Transport (now the Roads and Traffic Authority) would take care of the drivers' licences and vehicle registration papers and the Registry of Births, Deaths and Marriages would attend to the relevant certificates. Everything was done lawfully, under the provisions set up for witness protection.

Alteration of Sheik's physical appearance, such as the removal of his tattoos, was not considered until after his final appearances at court had been completed. There was no point in changing his appearance for all his brothers to see.

Podgorski was not the easiest of people to look after. He was young, selfish and did not enjoy the protection that he was being given. He wanted freedom and the choice of having a beer when he wanted. Podgorski had to be constantly reminded of the dangerous situation that he had created for himself.

He would play one shift of police officers off against one another by telling the oncoming shift that he had obtained prior permission to go out unsupervised. Although he didn't wash much, he fancied himself as God's gift to women. He would make advances to female police officers when he was alone with them.

Recreation was provided for him and his wife. Members of the Witness Protection Unit played golf and tennis with him, when the opportunity presented itself. Sheik usually won the tennis matches. Mrs Podgorski liked shopping. She could not be allowed to do this alone, however, and was always accompanied on these excursions by policewomen, who carried more than cosmetics in their handbags.

Sheik's parents were Polish immigrants who had a close relationship with their son. They were taken by the unit's members to secluded locations, where they would enjoy barbecues with him. Whenever Sheik and his wife dined out, which was not very often, they were escorted to out-of-the-way restaurants. The entire venue would be booked out by the unit.

During the court proceedings at Penrith, Podgorski's accommodation would sometimes be booked at motels closer to the court than Goulburn to save time and travel. Single-storey motels were chosen and a complete wing would be taken, with perimeter intrusion alarms set around the building. The fleet of police cars would be regularly changed to prevent familiarity and identification. Rented cars were also used as replacements.

Sheik was cocky at the start of his protection, but as time wore on and he came face-to-face with his former bikie brothers in court, he became very aware of their body language. The finger pointing in the shape of a gun and the clicking of fingers got through to him. He thought more and more about the situation in which he had placed himself and told his guards that he expected to get whacked. Sheik knew of the Nomad chapter of the Bandidos: the disciplinarians who were hunting him round the clock.

Bernie Podgorski's witness protection was maintained 24 hours of every day for over two years. Police performed two 12-hour shifts daily. At the completion of his evidence, Sheik and his family were taken to a secret location in country New South Wales, where they were placed in the future protection of officers from the Australian Federal Police. They became responsible for easing Sheik back into society unnoticed. Whether this would be interstate or overseas was never discussed with me. Boom Boom would remain the contact case officer in New South Wales.

Sheik's destiny and that of his family became his responsibility. He was a fugitive and could never return to his former life.

CHAPTER THIRTEEN

Halls of Justice

The defence lawyers made their applications to the court for separate hearings of their bikie clients. The applications were rejected. Instead, the court decided on a large, joint hearing of the case. Allan Viney, QC, would lead the prosecuting team, the antithesis of his previous defence role in the disjointed Bathurst Jail riots case. He was pleased with the result, being well aware of the problems that arose for the prosecution at Bathurst.

On 23 October 1984, the bikies' lower court hearing began at Penrith. It was the largest criminal case in the history of the Commonwealth. Coroner Greg Glass would take his place on the bench in the revamped court at Penrith Police Station to commence committal proceedings against 43 bikies charged with 301 counts of murder as well as the additional charges of affray.

Security arrangements surrounding the police station and court complex were stringent. The entrance to the station, off High Street, was under the supervision of uniformed police officers, checking the bona fides of anyone wishing to enter the building. The motor vehicle entrance to the rear, from Henry Street, was also defended from unauthorised entry. The basement car park was protected by a boom gate that was operated by a police guard. Rooftop patrols were filled by snipers from the Tactical Response

Group (TRG), who carried long arms as well as the departmentally issued revolvers.

Twelve uniformed officers stood guard across the front entrance to the court building, so that patrons were forced to enter in single file, passing through a magnetometer, a metal screening device similar to that seen at an airport. Keys and other metal objects were placed in a tray to pass through a separate X-ray device. Those people moving to the bikies' courtroom were physically searched before they could enter. A photography unit was established inside the entrance to the law courts, and people who were to attend court on a regular basis were photographed and issued with an identity card to be worn at all times while in the building.

An emergency alarm had been fitted to the coroner's bench which, if activated, would alert a small army of TRG reserve personnel on stand-by to action stations. In the event of a disturbance occurring in the court, such as a shooting, a contingency plan had been prepared, with each officer having a specific task. The coroner would be the first to leave, being quickly escorted from the bench by a personal bodyguard, followed by the Crown prosecutors. The courtroom would then be sealed and those people remaining inside would be left to defend themselves against the bikies and their cohorts.

The prisoners' dock was positioned in the centre of the courtroom and served as the entry and exit point for prisoners in custody being taken to court. The tunnel beneath the building connecting the courthouse to the police station was fitted with a series of alarm buttons in case of trouble during a prisoner transfer. Police usually place themselves in position well before any event and, by 9.30 am, they had been on duty at their posts for several hours. Human traffic began to increase as the 10 o'clock start approached.

The Crown team was the first to enter the courtroom, as protocol and propriety demanded. Senior counsel, empty-handed, were followed by junior counsel, followed by two solicitors. One of the latter juggled heavy law books and manuals, while the other guided a double-decker supermarket trolley holding the 'brief of evidence' into the halls of justice. The brief consisted of interviews, statements, photographs, plans and documents, bound together into 30 volumes. This mobile library would be wheeled from the police station to the courtroom and back every day.

Two detectives followed the lawyers, rolling a huge, custom-built gun rack mounted on wheels, carrying 47 weapons. Exhibits of firearms, baseball bats, club, iron bars, chains, knives and machetes were all contained in the structure, which resembled the wooden horse of Troy.

The prosecution benches were quiet and spacious. Not so the defence. Four Queen's Counsels, 19 barristers and 21 solicitors, plus law clerks, hustled for a prominent position while taking their seats behind three long tables extending across the width of the court. The associated paraphernalia brought by the lawyers filled the workbenches, leaving little room for the mandatory water decanter and glass.

Protocol was alive and well. I heard one QC remark to a court officer, 'Would you mind carrying my books into court? I'd be the laugh of Macquarie Street if I did it myself.' His clients would have understood this etiquette. They ordered their minions to carry their shotguns.

The clock in the bell tower of the Penrith Council Chambers struck ten. Like figurines emerging from behind a large Swiss timepiece, a door opened at the head of the courtroom and the bespectacled coroner appeared.

'This Court of Petty Sessions is now open,' called the court officer.

All the days of preparation were about to be tested. The arrests had been made, now it was time to prosecute.

The first two days of the committal proceedings were devoted to establishing the 'ground rules'. One by one, lawyers stood and announced to the court whom they represented. Then a decision on the order of merit in which each would cross-examine witnesses and address the court. Naturally, Queen's Counsels were victorious. They were at the head of the legal pecking order.

Then the coroner outlined to the legal fraternity how he intended to conduct the inquiry, a daily timetable and a projected hearing duration. Twelve months was the optimistic guess. An agenda was created, questions were to be answered. The court adjourned with the first witness to be called to give evidence on 12 November 1984, just 71 days after the bikies' war.

The Viking Task Force had a large office from which to work on the first floor of Penrith Police Station. Whiteboards covering the walls no longer contained information relative to police raids, but names of witnesses to be called at the lower court hearing. The logistics were mind-boggling: names and addresses, together with dates and times each witness would be called. The time the witness was warned to attend and whether a subpoena or warrant would be required to ensure his or her attendance. Four hundred names would eventually appear on those boards.

Adequate notice needed to be given to each witness concerning the date of his or her attendance. Many witnesses felt insecure about giving evidence in what was without doubt a very intimidating experience. Appearing in court under normal circumstances could be daunting, but before 43 bikies and a similar number of lawyers wishing to interrogate them was enough to make one's blood run cold. In many instances, it would be necessary for the task force to arrange suitable travelling arrangements for the deponents, with words of support offered en route.

A computer was installed in the task force operations room and, at the conclusion of each day's evidence, the transcripts would be brought from the court and entered into the database. Access to this information was available only to those officers not involved in giving evidence to the hearing. The progress of the inquiry could now be monitored to ensure a continuous and uninterrupted presentation of witnesses.

Two hundred police officers were available to give evidence, if required. They were stationed at many of the 30 police divisions that formed the geographical structure of the Sydney metropolitan police district. Expenses such as travelling allowance could be paid to officers attending court outside the metropolitan area for whatever period of time their presence at court was required.

No such allowance was available to officers if their court requirement was contained in the Sydney area, and Penrith was regarded as in the Sydney area. Although many kilometres away in distance and hours in time expended, no remuneration was made available. In most instances, an officer's evidence would take more than one day to recount, which meant several long and arduous journeys to and from court. The alternative was to remain at Penrith overnight at the officer's own expense, with no departmental allowances being provided.

We needed a way to overcome this problem. I approached Barney Ross with a suggestion that the department rent accommodation at Penrith on a short-term trial and a suitable three-bedroom house was found. An extra task would now be undertaken by Viking, that of stocking the kitchen cupboards with essential food items for the transient tenants.

The house would become a haven for police witnesses who, in those days, were compelled to recall their evidence from their powers of recollection. I remember a lawyer named Tony Bellanto making the most of this in the 'good old days'. Midway through his cross-examination of a police witness, he would ask, 'Are you relying on your memory in giving this evidence?'

'Yes,' replied the police officer.

'How good is your memory, Constable?' Bellanto asked.

'Very good,' the officer proudly responded.

'Well then, what was the fourth question I asked you in cross-examination today?' was his next question. Time and time again, the officers would be baffled.

Here, in a house away from the masses, there was time to prepare for court without interruption. Every police officer knows the feeling of pacing to and fro outside the courthouse, trying to memorise his or her lines, only to be distracted by an acquaintance in uniform who wants to catch up on the past.

Another distraction came from sources wanting to learn from our experiences. The Milperra Massacre had provided local and overseas media with saturation news coverage. Not only were journalists constantly requesting progress reports and accounts of police activity, but international law enforcement bodies were also taking an avid interest. The administration officers of the Bramshill Police College, a police training centre in London, requested a copy of the Hard Walk 84 operational orders, which they wished to include in their instruction manual. Observers from the FBI, Scotland Yard and countries where the tentacles of the outlaw bikie culture had invaded came to the task force office at Bass Hill to study and examine how police in Sydney were confronting the threat of bikie culture.

During all this time in 1984, I was the Commander of the Regional Crime Squad South, an attachment of the CIB. The department, in its wisdom, decided to upgrade the position to one rank higher. According to public service regulations, this meant my job was technically vacant and was now up for grabs to anyone who wanted to apply. The competition was intense.

In the middle of the biggest murder investigation in the history of the NSW Police Force came the added pressure of having to apply for my own job. The position was a promotion and I felt qualified for it. I submitted my written application and went before the selection panel – the Police Board. I was reappointed, now holding the rank of Detective Chief Inspector.

CHAPTER FOURTEEN

Witness Intimidation

At 6 am on 12 November 1984, two large police prison vans travelled from the city of Sydney, along Anzac Parade to the state penitentiary at Long Bay, Malabar. After a short drive through the outer perimeter grounds of the prison, the vans came to a halt outside the huge, intimidating steel doors enclosing the jail's population.

The activation of the buzzer on a masonry door pillar was answered by a uniformed prison guard. A lone police officer escort disappeared through a smaller doorway set into the much larger prison door. Seventeen consignment remand warrants were handed to the prison superintendent, and the Comanchero gang members were assembled in a caged compound, the transfer pen. They were laughing and seemingly nonchalant, trying to mask their apprehension. The bikies were on their way to court.

The two main doors of the jail were opened and the vans in turn backed up to the cage to receive their human shipment. Four police pursuit cars, each containing four heavily armed Tactical Response Group (TRG) officers dressed in black combat clothing, waited on the prison driveway.

At 6.30 am, the two vans had been loaded and, as they drove from the security of the jail onto the driveway, two police cars went to the head and two to the aft to form a convoy. The destination was Penrith, 60 kilometres away by air, but much further by road.

As would be the case of Sheik, the protected witness, the escorting vehicles with their emergency lights flashing and sirens screaming would daily pass uninterrupted through every set of traffic lights between Malabar and Penrith to safely deliver the bikies. A similar activity took place at the maximum security prison in Sunnyholt Road, Parklea. The distance of 25 kilometres was shorter for the Bandidos transfer. Their arrival at Penrith Police Station had to be completed before the appearance of the Comanchero. If the two gangs ever came face to face there would be another massacre.

As the vans arrived at their journey's end, they drove into the rear driveway of the police station, passing under the structure that held the prosecution team, through the opened boom gate and into the basement car park. There, the prisoners were handcuffed and, with police guards surrounding the vehicles, were removed and led to the receiving area in the cell complex. Each bikie was physically searched before being placed in the cell accommodation. Defence lawyers waited in the interview rooms for a final conference with their clients before each of them was presented to the court.

At 9.55 am, the bikies walked along the tunnel to a set of stone steps rising to a trapdoor. When opened, it would allow the prisoners to enter the courtroom. Once inside, the Comanchero would be mustered into an enclosure at the rear of the court, on the left-hand side. The Bandidos were on the right. Both gangs were in cages of bulletproof perspex.

At 11 am, the prisoners were escorted from the courtroom by the same route to the police cells, served with morning tea and scones and, 30 minutes later, returned to court for the resumption of the case. Similar breaks were taken for lunch. Four o'clock signalled the conclusion of the day's proceedings and the long journey home began.

Remand warrants had to be obtained by the escorting police from the clerk of the court to accompany the bikies on their return to the respective prisons. Without these warrants, the prisons would not readmit them.

The police convoys would then perform the morning's functions in reverse order. At 8 pm, the two vans and their crews drove in darkness along Anzac Parade towards the city, the day's duty for these officers completed. The crews from Parklea arrived back in the city at a similar time and parked their vans, ready for the task to be repeated once again the following day. This routine was followed every weekday for two years as the wheels of justice ground slowly.

The ground rules set by Mr Glass allowed the court to commence taking evidence immediately. At the beginning, on that November morning, Allan Viney, QC, delivered an oral summary of the events that would be covered in detail by Crown witnesses.

Dr Gregory Woods, QC, was instructed by junior counsel to appear in defence for a number of the Bandidos defendants. He typified the aura in the courtroom during his opening address to the coroner:

> This is the biggest, single criminal case ever conducted in
> Australian legal history, if not in the history of the common
> law world. Each defendant is charged with seven counts
> of murder which is probably unprecedented to have so
> many people charged with so many counts of murder. The
> incident in itself is described as one in which at the time
> the position was assessed, as being the largest investigation
> in the criminal history of the state.

Bernie Podgorski was soon thrown into the bearpit. He had been brought to Penrith Police Station from Goulburn early on the morning of 19 November 1984 by his Witness Protection Unit keepers. At 11.30 am, he was called to the court. Flanked by four

Special Weapons Operations Squad (SWOS) officers, observing a close personal protection pattern around him, he entered the courtroom. He was escorted to the witness box where he stood, now very much alone.

I could not be certain when the bikies first realised that Sheik had rolled over, but by this time everyone knew. The sound of stamping feet grew to a crescendo from both enclosures of bikie gang members. The shatterproof glass partitions did little to muffle the chorus of voices in rhythm chanting, 'Dead Meat, Dead Meat'. Podgorski had forfeited his gang name of Sheik and been given a new one by the brothers he had betrayed. They continued chanting 'Dead Meat' until brought to order by court staff.

As a member of both the Comanchero and Bandidos gangs, Podgorski was capable of identifying each offender, placing them at the massacre and relating to the court what part they had played. He also had knowledge of the war declaration and the hit list that had been compiled by the Bandidos.

All of his evidence was damning, but none more so than his revelation of Jock waving a machete above his head and shouting, 'Kill 'em all'. Here was the Supreme Commander, whose word was law to the Comanchero, ordering his men to kill. I could not think of a more significant action that would bond his men together in a joint enterprise of 'common purpose'.

Some defence lawyers were uneasy in their chairs, still doubting, or hoping, that Sheik would back down at the last hurdle. Not so solicitor Christopher Murphy. He was appearing on behalf of a number of Bandidos and was relishing the coming of an opportunity to cross-examine Bernie. Murphy was confident to the point of arrogance, and was well known for his ability to fight hard for his clients.

Podgorski was limited to some degree in his knowledge of the correct names of many of the defendants and relied on their gang names for identification. The bikies, sealed in their enclosures at the rear of the courtroom and without their Colours, were dressed in street clothing. Many had prepared for court by having their beards and hair trimmed. They looked almost respectable, quite different from their usual scruffy appearance, which always gave the impression they had just emerged from a brawl or a booze-up. 'Would you identify each defendant from your left to right?' asked the magistrate.

Podgorski hesitated and then started: 'Tiny, Bear, Lance, Chewey, Snoddy...'

Chris Murphy seized his first opportunity. He hurriedly rose to his feet from the bar table and interrupted Podgorski's evidence with a tactic many observers thought might terrify him to the state of being incapable of continuing.

'Your Worship,' he said, halting Podgorski in his identifications. 'The witness is being asked to identify these men from quite a distance away and he is keeping his head down. Could he be brought to the rear of the court in order that there can be no mistake and we might hear him better?'

Murphy's request was approved by Coroner Glass. Podgorski, visibly shaking, was led by a court attendant to the dock areas holding the bikies, the brothers he had betrayed. Here, for the first time since he had rolled over, he came face-to-face with the bikies and was asked to identify them.

Chris Murphy's attempt to silence Podgorski seemed to have succeeded. He stood silently, staring into the dock holding his former Bandidos brothers. The glares and gestures that passed from the bikies to their accuser could be seen by all present in the court. No words needed to be said, the hatred expressed in the bikies' body language almost fogged the perspex.

But the thought of immunity from prosecution was more appealing to Podgorski than joining his brothers in the dock. He started with, 'Tony', as he identified his former friend to whose son he was godfather. The moment of truth had passed. Bernie Podgorski would continue with his damning evidence for a further three months.

During his cross-examination, Sheik was asked if he relied solely on his memory to support his recollection of the events leading up to the massacre.

'No. As Secretary, I recorded the minutes of the meeting in writing,' he replied.

A red book lay on the bar table before Chris Murphy. 'How did you record those matters?' Murphy asked him. 'In the Minutes Book,' came Podgorski's reply.

'And where is that book?'

'That's it on your table,' said Podgorski confidently.

A jubilant Allan Viney sprung to his feet and exclaimed, 'I call for that book to be entered as an exhibit.'

The bikies' lawyers looked on, horrified. The book had finally been located, but in the most unusual and unexpected set of circumstances. It had apparently been given to Murphy by his clients and mistakenly taken to court by his assistant.

Podgorski endured intense cross-examination from the hordes of defence lawyers. Strong suggestions came from all quarters that he had been induced by the police to give his evidence, that it had been obtained by threats to his family and by false promises made to him. There was also a suggestion that he had been paid money by the prosecution. These allegations were made in an attempt to have his evidence withheld.

Sheik remained steadfast, denied the accusations and never wavered in the fact that he was the one who applied for indemnity, that the police had advised him that they did not need his evidence. His legal counsel would support all this if the defence wished to call him as a witness. They didn't.

Podgorski was not the only witness to suffer from nerves. A series of incidents occurred that did nothing to calm those who were to testify after him. A civilian witness associated with the bikie gangs received several anonymous threatening phone calls at his home. Then one afternoon, as he left a hotel in Berala in Sydney's west, he was shot in the leg by an unknown gunman.

Groups of Comanchero members from diverse chapters gathered in the street near the entrance to the court and directed looks of admonishment towards witnesses waiting to give their evidence.

Comanchero member Anthony John 'The Rat' Brennan had not been involved at Milperra as he was completing a 10-year jail sentence for the shotgun death of a bikie who had broken club regulations. On his release from prison, however, he became a familiar figure in the public gallery of the court. Witnesses who knew the Rat and his reputation voiced their uneasiness at his presence. His attendance at the court ceased when it was brought to his attention that associating with Comanchero brothers may have been a breach of his parole conditions.

Three female witnesses complained to members of Viking Task Force that they had received phone calls threatening them with murder and pack rape. The calls were anonymous, making the task of identifying them a virtual impossibility. More anonymous telephone calls, this time to the home of Mr Allan Viney, QC, left him and his family with the uneasy knowledge that his home had been located.

Michael and Deidre Langley were the joint licensees of the Viking Tavern on Father's Day 1984. After they gave their evidence to the court, they changed their employment and moved. The Tavern was a bikie's pub and they were scared of reprisals.

Bernie Podgorski's parents were listed in the telephone directory and they too became the subject of nuisance telephone calls. Clusters of motorcyclists would halt intermittently outside their home during the night, revving the motors of their machines before burning rubber on the roadway as they sped away. The loud, sudden noises terrified Sheik's parents. When a detective from the task force command was away from home, his wife and young child, alone in the house, were buzzed by the bikies as well.

Near the Christmas break I received a phone call at the Viking Task Force office from an unidentified male caller: 'Your Christmas present is running late, but don't worry, it will be a surprise. You won't know what it is or when to expect it.'

A most serious threat, however, was an attempt by a number of bikies to find out where Sheik was being housed. On several occasions, when they were leaving the Penrith complex with Podgorski, the SWOS protection group had noticed a series of motor vehicles following them. Evasive driving had stopped the would-be stalkers each time, but it was evident that different tactics needed to be employed.

So a series of 'dummy' runs began. Teams of police impersonating Podgorski and the SWOS teams would drive off in different directions, confusing the bikies and throwing them off the scent.

An emotional edge had developed in the minds of many people associated with the court case. While we could not prove that the bikies in the dock were responsible for these threats, feelings of apprehension had been created in the witnesses. And they knew what these bikies were capable of. They had seen it close up and bloody.

Snoddy, President of the Bandidos, was not spared the malevolence of a sardonic well wisher. On Valentine's Day 1985, a greeting card was mailed to him at Parklea Prison. It read: 'Happy Valentine's Day Snoddy. Wish you were here with me. Love Leanne.' It message referred, of course, to Leanne Walters, the massacre's youngest victim. It was meant to goad him and to strike at any sense of regret the Bandidos leader might have.

Under normal circumstances, Snoddy would have treated the card with scorn. But these weren't normal times. His gang had been decimated and most of its survivors were held in prison. Snoddy must have blamed himself for the destruction of his gang. The President and founder of Bandidos, Australia, was plagued with remorse and regret. In the hours he spent alone in his cell, he brooded on his failures and the damage he had done to the bikie brotherhood worldwide. Not surprisingly, he began to lose

his sanity. Cell 3233 in Wing Three of Parklea had been home
to Snoddy since his arrest in September 1984. He had proved to
be an artist with modest talent when he decorated the walls with
drawings of the fat Mexican, the Bandidos motif, surrounded
by the epithets, '1%', 'Bandidos Forever, Forever Bandidos' and
'FTW' (Fuck the World). He kept a diary in which he recorded his
feelings, frustrations and the future of his gang. The entries began
with the hope of acquittal on all charges, but when this failed to
eventuate, they began to degenerate into extreme despair. His
despondency was clear in this extract:

> We are the people that have not been in jail before and
> they put us in the most max jail in NSW. All it will do to
> us, well 'me' anyway is make me bitter towards the people
> that put me here. My mind is starting to crack, I just don't
> understand what is happening to us. I don't know how
> much longer I can hang on to my sanity. I wish we could
> get bail soon, it is sending me round the twist.

A few months later he wrote:

> I Tony Spencer
>   Do not want my wife to have any part in my life or
> death. Lee Denholm is my lady and Joel is my son &
> they get all my belongings. Lee I am sorry for this but
> remember I will always love you & my son.
>   Plus I want my bros to not think of me as week, but as
> fightin' for the well beeing of the club have fail mabe I
> don't know. But I do no some one will do the right thing
> for the club.

At 6 am on Sunday 28 April 1985, Snoddy was found dead, hanging
from the shower railing in his cell, a strip of white cloth knotted
around his neck. The body of the President was placed on his bed

and his fellow Bandidos inmates gathered in the cell to pay their last respects to another fallen brother. The massacre had claimed another victim. The trial was taking its toll on the survivors...

The bikie brief, although the major inquiry, was not the only matter in which task force officers were involved. One matter that concerned me was the Mick Drury bribery allegations.

The second departmental inquiry into suggestions of Roger Rogerson's attempted bribery of Drury involved witnesses who were now prepared to talk. Loyalty to Rogerson was beginning to falter. The Office of Public Prosecutions laid a charge of 'offer bribe' against the suspended detective.

A great deal of the evidence on which the Crown case was built came from the investigation by Angus McDonald and myself. I was asked to prepare a statement of the evidence that I would give at Rogerson's court hearing. Angus was not considered. He was left out in the cold, completely shunned by those in charge of the brief against Rogerson. The same applied to me to a certain degree. Other witnesses involved in the case were party to preliminary court conferences with the Crown prosecutor. I was excluded from the meetings. I accepted the snub as an affront to my integrity. Was I not to be trusted?

On 18 February 1985, I attended the Castlereagh Street local court and gave my piece of evidence. Rogerson was committed to stand trial. On 12 June, I attended the District Court, Sydney, where I gave my evidence at the trial of Rogerson. He was found 'not guilty' by the jury.

Perhaps now, this distraction could be put behind me and the job of presenting the bikie brief to the court could proceed without interruption.

* * *

Contrary to some public feeling, police officers do possess both a sense of humour and competitiveness. A sense of humour is needed in the force to maintain a responsible frame of mind, which is tested many times by a formidable, and often distasteful, assignment. A competitive edge is fashioned by the challenge to see that right will always be victorious over wrong.

The members of the task forces decided we would need our own emblem, or Colours, to identify us. Outlaw bikies identified themselves by the Colours they proudly wore and their open declaration to the community of being the 'one-per-centers'. The Task Force Colours should incorporate the events surrounding the massacre at the Viking Tavern as a symbolic reminder.

I sent out requests for an appropriate design. There would be no prize for the winner, only the satisfaction of knowing that a powerful symbol of justice had been created. We would wear our emblem on our tie. I also obtained a manufacturing cost from the clothing trade and called for tenders. An executive decision was made to sell the ties to members at double the manufacturing cost, the profits to be spent on a social celebration, if and when the trial ended. The ticket of entry to that event would be the wearing of the tie.

Many of the submitted designs would have done credit to Calvin Klein. The winner was a navy blue silk tie with the words 'Father's Day 84' in gold lettering at the point. A logo was positioned in the centre of the tie, consisting of the number '7' in red, representing the seven deceased, and a Viking helmet with the horns as the fulcrum of a set of scales depicted the Viking Tavern and the scales of justice, all in gold embroidery. Also in gold were '99%' under the left scale, representing members of the community, which outweighed the right-hand scale of a shotgun on wheels, depicting the weaponry and vehicles used by the bikies.

A total of 300 limited edition ties were sold, eagerly sought by both those involved in the prosecution as well as the defence. A search for a suitable venue to celebrate 'Tie Night' began.

The committal proceedings continued at the Penrith court, interrupted daily by the anonymous bomb hoax calls. At first they proved to have a disruptive effect, with the court being cleared of everyone including the prisoners. But as time went on, we decided the threats were hoaxes and ignored them.

The Office of Public Prosecutions within the Penrith courthouse building was burgled one night during a weekend recess. A fire was lit in the records area, but fortunately the fire was quickly brought under control after activation of the sprinkler system. No structural damage occurred, and no papers associated with the bikie matter were destroyed.

Looking after the bikies began to present additional logistical problems. Spartan Task Force consisted of police officers conducting transport from the jails as well as providing security at the court. Penrith Police Station held an average of six prisoners per day, but now with the 43 bikies being held there, the staff requirements increased by 300 per cent.

First the bikies had to be fed. This was done by a local caterer who won the tender to provide 'prisoners' meals' – another local business to profit from the Milperra Massacre. The members of the task force also had to be provided with food, this time by the Police Department. We had on previous occasions been able to use a mobile canteen. This canteen was the brainchild of the Cliff Rescuc Squad, which not only retrieved cliff and tall building jumpers but attended countless disasters, many lasting for some days. The Granville rail disaster had gone on for weeks.

The canteen was brought to Penrith and set up in the basement car park of the police station. There were no cordon bleu chefs, but most officers enjoyed pie and peas with plenty of sauce. I wondered what company had the contract of supplying the department with pies. They were on a goldmine. Very few police stopped at one.

Committal proceedings continued, witness intimidation continued, evidence of 'who hit who' continued – the only thing that changed was the weather. During winter at frosty Penrith I overheard one defence barrister flippantly say to a colleague,

'It really is winter. You can tell because the natives up here are wearing football socks with their thongs.'

I'd had enough of this crap from the lawyers. 'Put one of those socks in your gob, pal,' I told him. 'Some of our men are "natives" out here. Besides, they look no worse than you when you're wearing that horsehair wig.'

On 23 December 1985, after 14 months of lower court proceedings and just in time for Christmas, Mr Glass decided the bikies had a case to answer and committed each defendant to stand trial on all charges that had been proffered by the police.

Police officers, young and old, male and female, uniformed general duties, detectives and specialists, together with civilians, had endured lengthy and sometimes bitter cross-examination from the elite of the legal system to reach a milestone in common law history. The process had taken 14 months, but we were over the first hurdle. Now the entire matter would be repeated again in even greater detail before a judge and jury in the Supreme Court.

We had been given a breathing spell. The trial date had been set for April 1986, four months away. The bikies once again were refused bail in their applications to the courts, and now they would spend Christmas in custody. The morning ride to Penrith would stop and they would experience the monotony of jail life, unbroken by daily outings. Members of Spartan Task Force could catch up on their annual leave and rest days. We would have to be at our best for whatever lay ahead.

But the Viking Task Force had no holiday. In fact, the tempo of work increased. The embattled No. 1 Courtroom at Penrith had to be restored to its original condition for the trial to accommodate a jury. The Crown had occupied the jury box during the committal proceedings, and they would have to vacate that area for the jury.

There are two kinds of crime: a misdemeanour, which is dealt with as a summary matter; and a felony, which is treated as indictable. A summary matter can be heard and determined by a stipendiary magistrate in what was known as a Court of Petty

Sessions, but now renamed the Local Court. An indictable matter is determined by a judge and jury in the Supreme Court.

Murder is a felony, an indictable offence to be overseen by a judge. After an offender is charged with this offence, police prepare a brief of evidence, which is related to the magistrate in the lower local court. This is referred to as the committal proceedings. If the magistrate finds that a prima facie case has been established, he commits the defendant for trial at the higher Supreme Court. Otherwise the defendant is discharged. We had won round one, the committal for trial of the bikies.

In the case of a committal, the court papers are forwarded to the NSW Attorney-General. If the Attorney-General is of the view that a strong case exists, he or she will arraign the accused for trial. In the event of the finding that a reasonable jury, if properly instructed, would have difficulty in a finding of guilt, the Attorney-General will terminate the charge in what is called a 'no bill'.

At this time, during the recess, the papers for the 43 bikies were being considered by the Attorney-General.

There are no wigs or gowns worn at the lower court, everyone, except uniformed police and court officers, are dressed in mufti. The responsibility of prosecution at the lower court rested with the police. At the Supreme Court, however, the State Attorney-General directs the show through the office of the Director of Public Prosecutions.

The Milperra case was so large that the police were needed to assist its passage through the Supreme Court. The masses of witnesses had to be served with subpoenas by police. The court needed guarding and hundreds of participants would need protection. We were all soon part of the legal juggernaut which rumbled its way slowly, but inexorably towards a final verdict.

CHAPTER FIFTEEN

The Trial

Everyone had a busy Christmas, including the defence counsel. They used the break to prepare applications for the murder charges to be withdrawn. The Solicitor for Public Prosecutions considered the petitions and recommended to the Attorney-General the suspension of 11 of the charges. He found that the prosecution evidence would not convince a jury of the guilt of those 11 bikies to the charges of murder. However, the charges of affray would stick and proceed against them at a separate trial.

The end result was that 31 accused would stand trial at the Penrith Supreme Court, each charged with seven counts of murder and one charge of affray. The other 11 bikies charged with affray would follow at a later hearing.

With the respite between the two court hearings, the time seemed appropriate to observe 'Tie Night'. We chose an evening in March at the Rockdale Businessmen's Club in the St George district. The management of the club wished to demonstrate the public appreciation of the role played by the police and subsidised our contributions to ensure a successful function.

Three hundred ties filled the club premises. The night was filled with plenty of backslapping and reflections of amazement that we had come so far without any major hitch. But we still had a long way to go. Our ties were not ready to be put away just yet.

The bikies weren't the only ones with a fondness for uniforms, Colours and parades. Pomp and pageantry also accompanies legal matters in the NSW Supreme Court. There is no common street apparel there, but the black gowns and the battered wigs of the Queen's Counsels and barristers, differing only in the number of knots and curls in the formal dress. The more dishevelled the wig, the more it attests to surviving many courtroom battles.

The Honorable Justice Adrian Roden had been appointed as the trial judge and he would appear attired in a scarlet robe. Justice Roden had indicated the need to install a computer terminal for him to record the evidence and other matters of interest. Space would be required for this, and an operator. A tipstaff and personal attendants also needed accommodation on the bench, beside the judge. An extended library of law books was needed for the barristers. They also required a change room, where they could don their robes. The prosecuting team had fewer needs. They were housed in the carpeted, air-conditioned, demountable building high above everyone else.

As the trial was expected to last at least a year, an annual budget estimate was called for from all participating groups. Those figures were:

POLICE DEPARTMENT
    Investigation $1,000,000
    Trial security (Spartan) $1,600,000
Total: $2,600,000

PUBLIC PROSECUTIONS OFFICE
    Salaries of Crown prosecutors, legal officers and
support staff. Meal allowances. Junior counsel. Running
costs for hire cars. Witness expenses. Stores, stationery and
incidentals.
Total: $490,000

SUPREME COURT

Salaries of judge, associates, tipstaff, hire car, travel costs and allowances. Equipment (computer, facsimile etc) stationery and incidentals.

Total: $235,000

SHERIFF'S OFFICE

Jury fees, hiring of venue for empanelling, hiring of buses for jury transport and running costs, salaries of court officers.

Total: $483,000

LEGAL AID COMMISSION

Salaries as based on appointment of 16 public defenders.

Total: $1,200,000

GENERAL

Lease of additional accommodation for Crown prosecutors, public defenders and fit-out of leased premises.

Total: $165,000

Total estimates for twelve months: $5,073,900

The estimated length of the trial created a lot of concern because of the jury. Section 19 of the *Jury Act 1977* provided that criminal proceedings in the Supreme Court of the District Court in New South Wales would be determined by a jury consisting of 12 members. Section 22 of the Act states that where a member of the jury dies, or is discharged through illness, or any other reason, the trial could continue if the number of jurors is not fewer than ten. If it drops below ten, assent must be given by both the person prosecuting for the Crown and the accused.

During this lengthy trial, a real and distinct possibility existed that illness could strike the jury just when the trial was nearing completion. If it reduced the membership to below the authorised level, the trial would be aborted and we would have to start all over again. This was everyone's nightmare.

I submitted a proposal for consideration of amendments to the Jury Act. Under my proposal, the Crown prosecutor, if he deemed it to be appropriate, could recommend the empanelling of 15 jurors. The additional three would sit as reserves throughout the trial to fill any vacancy caused by any of the original 12 jurors dying or being discharged. This would be at the discretion of the trial judge.

A further amendment was proposed that the trial should be allowed to continue if the jury membership was reduced to nine people. Again, a discretionary power would rest with the trial judge concerning when this alternative procedure should be applied.

The suggestions seemed fair to all parties. The idea was forwarded but no decision was given prior to the commencement of the bikies' trial. It was a delay that could have proven disastrous. I wondered whether my proposal was not adopted because the submissions were made from a police officer and not one of the legal fraternity. Lawyers, like bikies, are conscious of their ranks and privileges.

Before a jury could be selected and empanelled, sufficient residents from the Penrith district had to be available. The defence had the right by law to challenge up to 20 persons called for jury service at the empanelling procedure: that is, jurors' names would be placed in a wooden selection box and one would be drawn from the box by the judge's associate. That person would then proceed to the jury box and, if the defence, or indeed the Crown, did not like the appearance or style of that person, they would say loudly 'challenge', before the person took the Bible to be sworn in.

The possibilities were alarming if each of the accused exercised his rights to the limit. As there were 31 prisoners being jointly tried, it was possible that 620 potential jurors might be challenged before one was selected. The Crown is permitted a similar right, so 1240 people could be required before a jury could be formed. This created a logistical nightmare.

Prospective jurors who were called for service and were unchallenged also had rights of appeal against selection. Any justifiable reason would be considered by the trial judge.

Notices for jury service were delivered to the eligible masses with a notice advising them that the trial in which they might be involved would be lengthy. Any reasonable excuse for exemption would be carefully and compassionately considered.

As soon as the potential jurors received this letter, they put two and two together and realised they were being considered for the Milperra Massacre trial. This revelation created great excitement for some, and terror and foreboding for others. Determining the fate of two gangs of outlaw bikies was not everyone's cup of tea. The returns were compiled at the local office of the Sheriff's Department, with eight thousand possible jurors being identified as available.

A little over a week remained before the start of the trial. Everything had been prepared. Security was in place. Witnesses had been forewarned about the dates they would be required and members of each task force had done the impossible and worked out rosters that would help them cope with the logistics of this massive legal event.

It was all going smoothly. Too smoothly. I had an uneasy feeling that something bad was about to happen. But when it did, even *I* was caught off-guard.

On 14 April 1986, I was in my office at the Remington Centre in Liverpool Street when I received a telephone call from a disgruntled police officer. He was never an associate of mine, yet the essence of his call was that he wanted me to stand up for him as a character witness. Maybe because I was a senior officer, my words might help him. I was not prepared to do what he asked and I told him so.

He became annoyed and said, 'If you don't, I'll bring your bikie brief down.'

'How could you do that? You don't know anything about it. You weren't involved,' I replied.

'I can make something up. It won't be hard. Either you do what I want or I'll do it,' was his disgusting threat.

My temper had been aroused and, after a tirade of abuse from me, I hung up on him. I recorded the conversation and later that morning I met with Police Commissioner John Avery and informed him of the phone call. I then sought advice from prominent lawyer Rick Burbidge, QC, and accepted his opinion that if there was a repetition of what had taken place, a charge of 'attempt to pervert the course of justice' could be considered.

The threat, however impracticable it appeared at the time, obviously caused me concern. We had enough opposition from the bikies and their legal representatives without any from our former officers.

A troublemaker may be able to create enough doubt in the minds of the jurors to be able to damage a brief. What else could he do? Start rumours? Intimidate witnesses? The possibilities ran through my mind. A liar can cause devastation to anybody.

I wondered whether this was the person who had threatened Angus McDonald when we were inquiring into the Mick Drury bribery allegations. I didn't want to ask him again when he had decided to remain silent. The bikies had Podgorski. We had our own snake in the grass.

Despite the extra worry, nothing eventuated from this menace. To this date, I have never heard from or spoken to this person again.

Monday 28 April 1986 was the first day of the trial. Justice Roden was escorted to the bench by his tipstaff. A court official proclaimed the sitting of the Supreme Court in session.

The 31 accused bikies stood independently in the respective Comanchero or Bandidos enclosed dock as their names were called and the charges read by the judge's associate. The 248 indictments of murder took 30 minutes to read:

'William Ross. You stand indicted that on the second day of September in the year one thousand nine hundred and eighty four, at Milperra in the State of New South Wales, you did feloniously murder Leanne Walters.'

That was just one charge, another six were to follow for Jock. The same procedure was repeated for the remaining bikies: Anthony 'Lard' Melville, Ian 'Snow' White, Glen Eaves, Robert 'J.J.' Heeney, Raymond 'Sunshine' Kucler, Colin 'Caesar' Campbell, Stephen 'Opie' Cowan, Ray Denholm, Phillip 'Bull' Campbell, James 'Roach' Posar, Gregory 'Dukes' McElwaine, Mark 'Gloves' McElwaine, William 'Davo' Littlewood, Charlie Scibberas, Tiny Cain, Lance 'Kid Rotten' Purdie, Mark 'Junior' Shorthall, Graeme 'Wilko' Wilkinson, Louie Cooper, Stephen 'Bear' Roberts, Lance Wellington, Scott 'Bones' Dive, Michael 'Tonka' O'Keefe, Kevork 'Kraut' Tomasion, Richard 'Chewey' Lorenz, James 'Mort' Morton, Terry Parker, Gary 'Peewee' Annakin, John 'Littlejohn' Hennessey and Phillip 'Knuckles' McElwaine.

A plea of 'not guilty' was entered by each accused.

The Queen's Counsels, barristers and the solicitors then identified themselves to Justice Roden.

Penrith Rugby League Club, on Mulgoa Road, just two kilometres from the courthouse, had opened early that morning, not as a special favour to the members, but to receive the number of local residents who had been called for jury service. An initial group of three thousand possible jurors gathered at the club, waiting to be called to the buses in the car park. The buses would take them to the court, 50 at a time.

When the call came from the sheriff at the courthouse, the first bus load departed for the court. They disembarked at the entrance to the court complex, then passed through the metal detector frame on their way to Courtroom No. 1.

One by one, their names were called in the presence of the accused and the Crown. One by one, the challenge came. A bus load of rejected jurors was taken from the court and a fresh consignment brought in.

One man who did not want to serve, but who did not have a valid excuse for exemption, had an ingenious idea. When his name was called, he strode confidently towards the jury box, then stopped and nodded to a uniformed police officer, saying loudly, 'Hello Pete.' He was immediately challenged by the defence as being a biased juror. So he walked from the courtroom smiling. He didn't know 'Pete' from a bar of soap. Groans and sighs of disappointment came from the bikies when attractive young women were challenged by counsel and rejected. At the conclusion of the day, five jurors had been accepted and sworn in, 203 had been turned away.

On the second day two of the empanelled jurors produced medical certificates and asked to be excused. The judge discharged them, as well as the other three, so the process started again from scratch.

Justice Roden was not impressed and commented, 'You have probably often heard it said that the law is an ass. No one knows better than those who work in it.'

A bearded man was called, but wailed that he couldn't afford to be on a jury, so he was rejected. A woman sobbed, 'I don't want to do it'. She was dismissed.

Three days passed before the six-male, six-female jury was selected and empanelled. Seven hundred people had been turned down and they, with the remaining seven thousand, breathed a sigh of relief as they collected a total of $96,800 in attendance money and returned to their normal lives.

The 12 'good and true' jurors were formally greeted by Justice Roden, who advised them that it was their duty to listen to the evidence and leave the rules of law to him. They then retired for the first time to select their foreperson.

The sheriff at Penrith was a far cry from the Wyatt Earp of early American Western history. This modern-day officer's duties involved supplying the Supreme Court with attendants and looking to the welfare of the jurors. The 12 jurors just selected had suddenly acquired VIP status and were his to supervise and nurture over the ensuing months. His human relations skills would be fully tested.

Provided with an advance account of $50,000, he would select and provide a variety of meals to satisfy the tastes of the dozen. Sometimes takeaway food was brought in. On other occasions, the jurors dined out at the finest a la carte restaurants in the area.

When they ate out, it was always under the close protection of the sheriff's officers, equipped with two-way portable police radios in case of an emergency or interference.

The pressure would become even more intense when the jury began to deliberate on their verdicts. Before this, each member at least had the nightly comfort of home, but when the time came to consider their judgments, they would be 'locked up'. The top floor of a local motel would become their common home and would be the subject of a 24-hour, seven-day strict security operation.

During the lengthy trial, the sheriff was to be faced with additional and unexpected problems, such as the provision of a staff member for childminding duties during one juror's family emergency. He also had to cope with escorting jurors to hospital to visit sick relatives, and even giving marriage guidance because of the trauma associated with the disrupted lifestyle. The $70 per day payment to each juror for his or her significant role in the judicial system seemed totally inadequate.

Witnesses who had given evidence at the lower court proceedings once again testified to the events that occurred at the Viking Tavern on Father's Day. Meanwhile, members of both bikie gangs who were not charged dressed in their Colours and gathered in separate locations near the Penrith court to scowl at those waiting to give evidence. The Viking Task Force was tested again by the extra duties of having to provide transport to those suffering anguish from the ongoing court ordeal.

To his credit, the trial judge controlled the proceedings with fairness, delicacy and artful management. He also showed a sense of humour that brightened the sometimes mundane debates on points of law. A former editor of the University of Sydney students' magazine *Honi Soit* and an exceptional debater, Justice Roden quickly showed that he would not allow the trial to develop into an endurance event. His remarks to lawyers included, 'When you rise, say something, don't just talk, otherwise the trial will take twenty years', and, 'Why did the committal proceedings take so long? Wasn't the magistrate there?'

On another occasion, in a light-hearted overruling of an objection made in the absence of the jury, the judge remarked that a 'cry wolf' syndrome was developing and that, 'One of these days a valid objection might be made and I might miss it'.

The Viking Task Force worked tirelessly behind the scenes to ensure the free flow of all evidence to be placed before the jury. A timetable of witness attendance was strictly adhered to, with no interruptions to the ongoing parade.

What do prisoners do in jail to pass the time? Some read, some write books, some paint, and some develop the prison yard walk. Comanchero Raymond 'Sunshine' Kucler decided he'd pump iron. But his love of muscle-building nearly ruined the entire trial. After several months, his hobby turned to obsession and he soon resembled a human tank.

A well-known violent criminal under remand in the same wing at Long Bay befriended the bikie powerhouse and commissioned him as his minder. Soon after, Sunshine became involved with a plot to seriously assault another prisoner. Fortunately the plan failed, and those behind it found themselves charged with conspir-acy. The Comanchero and his co-conspirators were taken to Central Police Station to await a court hearing before a Sydney magistrate.

Jim Tutill was a uniformed NSW Police inspector and had been placed in charge of the Spartan Task Force. The bikie trial had been going on for several weeks when Jim came to me one morning while I was at Penrith.

'Ron, a bit of a problem,' he started. He stopped momentarily as he performed a giant drawback on the cigarette held between his teeth. I watched, thinking the smoke would come out his ears.

'One of the bikies didn't turn up this morning.' 'Why not? What happened?' I asked.

'He got nicked for another charge and he's gone to Central. I suppose he reckons another matter won't get him any more than seven murders,' Jim said in a carefree manner, obviously not appreciating the seriousness of the problem the bikie had created for our trial.

'He should be at Penrith in front of the jury, not at Central in front of a magistrate. Who is it?' I asked.

'Sunshine Kucler,' Jim replied.

His absence was disturbing to say the least. Members of the press, the police roundsmen and women and the court reporters would all be waiting at Central to report to the world that one of the Comanchero bikies was facing another serious charge. The Penrith trial, could, or would be, aborted. The jury would be discharged and the whole circus might have to restart from scratch.

I informed Justice Roden of the situation and then made an urgent telephone call to the NSW Police Prosecuting Branch at Central. Fortunately, I was able to speak to Frank McGoldrick who had been involved with the bikie investigation. I asked him to delay Kucler's appearance in court until I arrived.

Sunshine was already in 'the slot', a holding room off the No. 1 Courtroom at Central from where prisoners in custody would emerge to face the magistrate. Frank removed Kucler from the 'launching pad', but then another realisation hit: a charge of conspiracy required the names of the plotters to be recorded on the court's charge sheets. Even with the non-appearance of the bikie, his name would be called in open court when the charges against his co-conspirators were read out. It would not take long for the court reporters to work out Kucler's identity and his connection with the bikie trial.

The charge sheets were retyped, leaving out Sunshine's name. He would be charged separately and face an in camera or closed court hearing and be remanded to a future date when that charge could be determined.

Everything worked out fine. Just another hiccup in the process to overcome.

* * *

Another New Year came and went, and vacancies arose in the department. I applied for the position of Detective Superintendent in Charge of Operations at the CIB and got the job.

The bikie hearing was like a war, hours of boredom and moments of terror. Many periods of time in court were spent listening to discussions on points of law. Then there was the apprehension of an attack during the transfer of the bikies back to jail. The energy of both the Spartan and Viking task forces began to wane. Travelling the same road to the same court for two years did have a way of testing the patience of everyone concerned, including the bikies.

Then, out of the blue, our worst nightmare occurred, just as I predicted at the start of the trial. One of the jurors failed to appear at the hearing. He had been struck down with hepatitis, a highly contagious illness. How far had the virus spread? Were other jurors infected? The juror had to withdraw. A terrible question hovered in the air: could the trial continue?

Justice Roden decided that he would go on with a panel of 11 jurors. We all kept our eyes on the remaining jurors for any signs of failing health.

Bernie Podgorski had testified for the second time, once again relating the involvement of the accused bikies in the massacre. Again, he came under intense cross-examination from defence lawyers and an equal concentration of rancour from his former brothers.

Once his evidence was complete, the Crown no longer had to look after Podgorski on a daily basis pending any appeal that might be forthcoming. Suggestions had been made in the media that Sheik was paid money to roll. He didn't receive one cent, let alone 30 pieces of silver.

The pressure not only lifted on Podgorski, but also his bodyguards. For almost two years, the Witness Protection Unit had chaperoned their guest for his court appearances and during his private life. Sheik possessed all the desires of a high-spirited male, a bikie, a person who had been active in wild living, drinking sprees and self-indulgence. He wasn't tamed readily.

Now this time had ended and Bernie Podgorski no longer existed. As John Citizen, he would be deposited at a location unknown to me, to live or die as a quisling.

CHAPTER SIXTEEN

The Verdicts

The witnesses had given their evidence and been professionally cross-examined before the jury. The Crown and defence had delivered their submissions in the summing up process.

Justice would now be delivered.

Before commencing his summary of evidence to the jury, Justice Roden outlined how he intended to announce the verdicts. He would summarise the case against each of the bikies separately and then he would ask the jury to retire and reach a verdict in respect of that bikie only. The foreman of the jury would place the written verdict in a sealed box without announcing the decision.

The judge would then proceed to the next bikie, and so on, until all verdicts had been reached. The jury would be given the opportunity to reconsider any verdicts if they felt it necessary.

Justice Roden's oral address was aided in the interpretation by a prepared document handed to each member of the jury. The document read:

The Four Questions:
1. Was he party to the fight?
2. If so, was he unlawfully party to the fight?
3. If so, was he unlawfully party, not only to the fight, but to the shooting that caused death?

4. Is so, did he act with the intention or state of mind necessary for his offence to be murder?

What They Mean:
1. Was he party to the fight?
Means:
(a) Did he participate in the fight? or
(b) Did he intentionally assist or encourage any of those who did? or
(c) Was he present, ready to help if required, having agreed to do so?
Any of the three is sufficient.

2. Was he unlawfully party to the fight?
Means:
His part in the fight would be unlawful, unless it is justified on the self-defence principle.
That requires what he did, or what he assisted or encouraged, or agreed to help, was done for the purpose of defence against an unlawful attack only, and that the violence used was reasonable in all the circumstances.

3. Was he unlawfully party, not only to the fight, but to the shooting that caused death?
This requires in the circumstances of this trial, that he knew or expected that guns would be used.

4. Did he act with the intention or state of mind necessary for his offence to be murder?
That is:
(a) That he himself intended that a person or persons be killed or really seriously injured; or
(b) That he knew those he was assisting or encouraging, or whom he agreed to help, had such intention; or

(c) That he realised that death might well result.

The Process
    1.   Pose the first question.

        Was he party to the fight – If you are not satisfied beyond reasonable doubt that he was, in one of the three ways explained, acquit on all charges. If you are satisfied, pass to Question 2.

    2.   Was he unlawfully party to the fight?

        If you are not satisfied beyond reasonable doubt that he was, acquit on all charges.

> If you are so satisfied, consider the Affray charge and, if you are satisfied beyond reasonable doubt that the nature of the fight to which he was party was such as might reasonably be expected to terrify a person of reasonable firmness, convict of Affray, if not satisfied, acquit on the Affray charge.

For the purpose of the Murder charges, pass to Question 3.

    3.   Was he unlawfully party, not only to the fight, but to the shooting that caused death?

> If you are not satisfied beyond reasonable doubt that he did, you cannot convict of murder, but you will convict of manslaughter if you are satisfied beyond reasonable doubt that the unlawful shooting to which he was a party was dangerous.

> If you are so satisfied, you will convict of murder, unless a manslaughter verdict is appropriate by reason of excessive self-defence or provocation.

> In respect of all matters, a conviction requires proof beyond reasonable doubt.

The jury retired a total of 31 times to consider individual verdicts. It took the panel of jurors 90 hours of deliberation before their final decisions would be given.

Those verdicts were delivered on Friday 12 June 1987. The courtroom was filled to capacity, with reserved seats only in the public gallery containing police, media representatives and selected relatives of the accused who had maintained a daily vigil throughout the trial. The foyer of the court complex was partitioned to form an enclosed area for the members of the public, adjacent to Courtroom No. 1, with a sound system provided for the overflow of people to hear the outcomes.

As it was impossible to predict the reaction from the accused and friends if the decision went against them and convictions were recorded, security in the cells below, in the courtroom itself and in the temporary public gallery had been dramatically increased for this day.

Information from Spartan Task Force security reported that the bikies were 'itchy'. The Tactical Response Group officers were dressed in their black combat gear and carried long batons close to their sides. Thirty-one bikies could provide formidable opposition. I sat in the mezzanine public gallery, watching the spectacle below. Everyone appeared nervous, with little conversation passing between lawyers and court officials. Then came the entry of the bikies. They nodded to a relative in the gallery and gave an uneasy smile.

Almost three years had elapsed since the futile war of Father's Day 1984. The results of the police investigation would now be determined. I felt nervous as I recalled the words of Barney Ross in the beginning: 'You started it, you finish it.'

The panel of jurors filed into the jury box for the last time. The bikies stood until the jurors had been seated. I looked at the faces of the jurors for an indication of their decisions. From my experience after attending many trials, I had learned that if the jury look at the accused, they would acquit. Not one of the panel looked towards the two enclosures holding the 31 bikies.

The judge's associate rose and faced the jury. 'Would the foreman please stand?' she asked.

A youngish man, his hair tied back in a ponytail similar to those whose future now rested with his announcement, rose.

'Members of the jury. Have you reached your verdicts?' was the question of the moment.

'We have,' replied the foreman in an unwavering voice.

Everyone held their breath. Not a sound was heard in the courtroom.

Then came the verdicts. Individually, each accused heard his fate as he stood in the prisoners' dock.

'Guilty of seven charges of murder, guilty of affray' or 'Not guilty of murder, but guilty of seven charges of manslaughter and affray'. The jury delivered a total of 63 convictions of murder and 147 convictions of manslaughter, with 31 convictions of affray.

Relatives and friends wept, sighed or just sat stunned. I felt a sense of overwhelming relief. All the efforts of the police involved had been rewarded.

After the jury foreman announced a unanimous agreement of each verdict, the judge's associate had the last word: 'So say your foreman, so say ye all'.

The prisoners were removed from the court to the cells below, quiet and numbed, the sting had been taken out of them. Now, having been found guilty, they were left to ponder what penalty would be imposed.

The bikies had been remanded for two weeks, until Friday 26 June 1987, for sentencing, with one exception: Bandido Phillip 'Knuckles' McElwaine, a former Commonwealth Games boxing gold medallist. Knuckles suffered from physical and psychological impairments, the legacy of a motor vehicle accident. He had been convicted solely of the charge of causing an affray. A conviction of this type carried no statutory penalty. That was left to the discretion of the judge. On this occasion, Knuckles was released after entering into a recognisance to be of good behaviour for two years. As he left the court, he no doubt reflected on the destiny of his real-life brothers Gregory 'Dukes' McElwaine and Mark

'Gloves' McElwaine, both Bandidos who had been convicted of seven counts of manslaughter and one of affray.

Before the jury was discharged, Justice Roden thanked the visibly weary panel for their attention during the marathon trial, which had achieved something that many people had thought impossible. He commented that their continued good health had saved a lot of public money and embarrassment.

In a final quip, His Honour referred to the outdated rules of evidence and court procedure which did not allow the jury to read certain evidence and submissions which, 'suggested that jurors can't read and that judges can't write'.

On 15 June 1987, Justice Roden began receiving oral and written submissions from the defence lawyers on matters of penalty and mitigating circumstances. This would be their only chance to make a credible appeal for leniency, a tough task.

On 26 June 1987, the 30 bikies returned to the Penrith court for the last time. The journeys from Long Bay and Parklea Prison would end after that. They were taken from the cells, along the tunnel and up the stairs into the courtroom to await the decision of Justice Adrian Roden.

In his 17-page decision, His Honour replied to the requests and pleas that had been submitted by the defence lawyers. He read the decision aloud before proceeding to sentencing. Selected passages of his judgment sketched the futility of the Father's Day war and probably the often asked, but unanswered question, 'Why did it have to happen?'

> *Throughout the sentence hearing, I sought a greater understanding than I was able to obtain of the nature of the clubs and the relationship between their respective members.*
>
> *There was, I thought, a very good reason for that. Some are in their thirties and forties, have no significant prior convictions and have good family and work backgrounds. I*

felt that there had to be some explanation for the marked
and perplexing difference between their behaviour in
other contexts. I also wanted to know more about the clubs
themselves and what it is about the way of life that they
offer that led these people, many of whom would in all
other respects be regarded as law abiding and responsible
citizens of commendable character, to indulge in what
on the face of it is irresponsible, anti-social behaviour
of extreme violence, bringing with it obvious danger
to human life, and in the facts of this case, the tragic
consequences of seven deaths.

It is not possible to sit looking at these men for more
than one year, as I have done, without feeling that there
is more to them than the popular image of bikie gang
members. It is unfortunate that so many of them have
chosen to play no part in the sentence hearing, although
years of their lives are at stake.

A fierce loyalty and a propensity for violence, which
rightly or wrongly typify the popular image of such
clubs are clearly indicated by the almost intimidatory
appearance adopted, and the emphasis on strength and
power to be found in man and machine alike.

A need to belong and enjoy a close relationship and
bond with others can be readily understood. So can a pride
in physical strength and courage. But like most admirable
qualities, these can be carried to excess. The ugly side to
loyalty seems to demand enemies against whom the loyal
can be united, and the ugly side to physical strength and
courage is seen when violence is unleashed against those
enemies. When you have two groups like these in conflict
with one another, a 'Viking' is always likely.

As patriotism can lead to jingoism and mateship can
lead to cronyism, so bikie club loyalty, it seems, can lead to
bikie club war.

In assessing sentence, it is appropriate to treat all the
offences of which any accused was convicted of as part
of the one transaction. It is proper to have regard to the
totality of the criminal conduct of which each had been
convicted and then sentence accordingly. The fact that
seven people were killed is itself a significant, aggravating
circumstance as is the fact that there were hundreds of
people whose lives were put at risk.

I now turn to deal with each of the prisoners separately.

As each prisoner's name was called, he stood in the dock to receive his sentence.

Lard Melville, Snow White, Glen Eaves, J.J. Heeney, Terry Parker, Peewee Annakin, Littlejohn Hennessey, Sunshine Kucler and Jock Ross each received life sentences in respect of their murder convictions and concurrent sentences ranging from 16 years down to 10 years for causing affray.

The remaining bikies convicted of seven charges of manslaughter and one charge of affray – Caesar Campbell, Opie Cowan, Ray Denholm, Bull Campbell, Roach Posar, Dukes McElwaine, Gloves McElwaine, Davo Littlewood, Charlie Scibberas, Tiny Cain, Kid Rotten Purdie, Junior Shorthall, Wilko Wilkinson, Louie Cooper, Bear Roberts, Lance Wellington, Bones Dive, Tonka O'Keefe, Kraut Tomasion, Chewey Lorenz and Mort Morton – received sentences ranging from 10 years to 14 years, with the affray convictions warranting concurrent sentences of seven years.

The prisoners were removed from the court to await transport to prison. It was the last they would see of the outside world for years.

The courtroom and adjacent areas that had been set aside for the public slowly emptied for the last time. Police, lawyers, court officials, sheriff's officers, bikie supporters, friends, relatives, members of the media and countless other spectators, all departed. The legal juggernaut had at last come to a halt. The Milperra Massacre was now part of history.

I broke the silence and said to the prosecution team, 'Let's have a drink. My shout.'

CHAPTER SEVENTEEN

Did Anyone Learn?

On 30 July 1987, I attended a passing out parade of fresh-faced police recruits at the NSW Police Academy in Goulburn. Several hundred newly attested police officers stood at attention in their lines before the parade commander, NSW Police Commissioner John Avery.

I was escorted by an aide to where the Commissioner was standing and, after exchanging salutes, he handed to me a framed Commissioner's Commendation.

'Well done, Ron,' he said, as we shook hands and I accepted the award from him.

Written on the certificate were the words:

Awarded to Detective Superintendent Ronald Harry Stephenson in recognition of his outstanding leadership and command of the police resources concerned with the investigation of the 'Father's Day Massacre, Milperra' on 2 September 1984. The Detective Superintendent's ability in controlling and co-ordinating this inquiry, contributed to the successful outcome of this matter which brought considerable merit to the nsw police force.

J K Avery, Commissioner of Police

That was my recognition, greatly treasured, but I was really receiving it on behalf of my teams: the two hundred police officers, male and female, young and old, senior and junior in ranks who had carried out my orders and, with their individual initiative, achieved an extraordinary result. They too were entitled to have their efforts recognised.

I returned to my Sydney office and, over a period of time, gathered the names of every police officer involved in the investigation and where he or she was now stationed. No matter how small or how large their contribution, each officer formed part of the wheel that rolled to victory. They were all identified, in excess of 250 of them.

When an officer joined the NSW Police Force, all personal and departmental actions were recorded in a booklet called a Service Register. This register remained with that officer until his or her retirement from the job and recorded all their employment details. Items such as ammunition used, examinations completed, annual leave, sick leave, special abilities and salary were but a few. Two notations of significant value were recorded under the headings Complaints and Commendations. A standing joke among police officers was to finish your service with a level evenly balanced between the two.

I wrote to every officer involved, telling each one that a commendation would be listed in the Service Register. It was the least I could do for such a gallant group of officers.

The Milperra Father's Day Massacre investigation had been successful because of the dedication of the 250 police officers involved and the solid structure of a united NSW Police Force. Four months after the conclusion of the trial, that unity was shattered. The CIB was broken up and decentralised.

The staff of one thousand were allocated and transferred to the regions, approximately 250 to each. Some special crime squads were maintained regionally in a smaller manner, operating only within their respective region. Most squads were discontinued. It was impossible to work competently with their restricted numbers. The specialists were absorbed into general crime investigations. The expertise of the CIB was lost.

The Homicide Squad had a staff of one hundred qualified and trained investigators dedicated to the business of solving suspicious deaths, able to spend infinite hours on each investigation. After cost-cutting regionalisation, this number diminished to 25 officers in each region. With annual leave, rest days, sick leave, court commitments and ongoing murder inquiries, the effective strength at any one time could be no more than a dozen officers. This means it would be impossible to investigate more than three murders at a time, let alone handle the complexities of a terrorist investigation.

Statistics taken over many years showed that 100 murders per annum occurred within New South Wales. Dividing this evenly between the four police regions would give each region 25 murders to investigate each year. Criminality is now so complex that each case requires between five and 14 officers. In addition, crime has risen more than 720 per cent since 1996, but there are fewer officers available with the skill to manage complex cases such as mass conspiracy and murder. There would be no one left to assist in a murder inquiry as massive as Milperra.

The No. 19 Police Division is part of the southwest region, which would now become responsible for the investigation of another Milperra. Similarly, the south region would be responsible for the investigation of the terrorist bombings in Sydney and Bondi. To call for assistance from another region would now be met with a response, 'We have our own crime to look after, sorry we can't help. We might be able to let you have a couple of blokes for a few days.' Given that some crimes have risen by 1040 per cent in the last ten years, such a response is not as callous as it might seem. Resources can only be stretched so far before something snaps.

An appropriate task force could be established for the required investigation, but it would take time. And time is critical. Immediacy is the key word in crime solving.

Milperra sent us a message. But did anyone learn?

Epilogue

The release of this book coincides with the twentieth anniversary of the Milperra Massacre. The lives of the people involved in that event have changed, but the memories remain unaltered. I have never forgotten Milperra, or those police officers who followed me in that massive investigation.

The senior officers who formed my command group and stood with me outside the mobile command post in the car park of the Viking Tavern on that Father's Day are no longer serving police officers. In 1991 I retired from the NSW Police Force and remain an interested observer of the criminal events unfolding around us daily. Detective Sergeant Barry Smith was promoted to the rank of inspector before retiring to the life of a winegrower in the Hunter Valley district of New South Wales. Detective Sergeant Darryl Wilson also received promotion to commissioned rank in the force.

He retired recently after years of distinguished service to a more peaceful life in the NSW southern highlands.

Detective Sergeant Aarne Tees advanced to the rank of detective inspector. He studied law and passed his examinations with honours before induction into the Barristers and Solicitors Admission Board. Aarne left the force to practice privately as a successful barrister. His life was cut short in 2002, dying suddenly after a short illness.

Jim Counsel retired from the force in 1999, holding the rank of detective inspector. He remains a close friend. Bill Duff resigned from the force shortly after the conclusion of the Milperra trial. He held the rank of detective sergeant.

The remaining two hundred officers remember the part they played in the inquiry, more so when they glance at their Milperra tie, which is held in great respect. But what befell the bikies?

Each offender found guilty at the trial was sentenced by the court in accordance with his culpability in the massacre. Those sentences have been recorded elsewhere in this book. However, the actual amount of jail time served by each prisoner is of interest. The President of the Comanchero, 'Jock' Ross, served the longest period of detention: five years and three months. The rest of the bikies served an average time of four years and six months. I have been asked on many occasions whether I was disappointed with this result. My answer is that the punishment is not the role of the police officer. We successfully planned and brought the bikies to justice. That is our reward.

www.ingramcontent.com/pod-product-compliance
Lightning Source LLC
Chambersburg PA
CBHW072008090426
42740CB00011B/2144